# LIBERATION ETHICS

# Liberation Ethics

G E R A R D  F O U R E Z

**Temple University Press**  **Philadelphia**

Temple University Press, Philadelphia 19122
© 1982 by Temple University. All rights reserved
Published 1982
Printed in the United States of America

Originally published in French as
*Choix ethiques et conditionnement social*
by Editions du Centurion, 1979
© Editions du Centurion, 1979

This translation and adaptation prepared by
David Morris, Barbara Hogan, and Gerard Fourez.

*Library of Congress Cataloging in Publication Data*
Fourez, Gerard.
   Liberation ethics.
   Translation of: Choix éthiques et conditionnement
social.
   1. Social values. I. Title.
HM73.F6813  303.3'72  82-799
ISBN 0-87722-254-1  AACR2

# CONTENTS

Foreword                                                    vii
Preface                                                      xi
Acknowledgments                                             xv

**PART**    1 Taboos, Norms, Values                          3
**ONE**     2 Where Do Moral Codes Come From?              24
            3 The Production of Notions                     35
            4 Law—Justice and Society                       53
            5 Obligatory Morality or Amorality?             69

**PART**    6 Individual and Interpersonal Ethics           99
**TWO**     7 Emotional Relationships in a Given Society    125

**PART**    8 The Ethics of Collective Issues               177
**THREE**   9 Capitalism and Socialism                      189
           10 Realism or Utopia? Conviction or
              Responsibility?                                205
           11 The Individual and Structural Questions       218

# FOREWORD

American readers may find Professor Fourez's style of ethics unfamiliar. That is because ethicists in this country have in general remained distanced from the insights of Karl Marx. This is not at all the case in Western Europe, nor is it the case in South America. There, ethicists, whether religious or secular, begin by presupposing that unveiling the relationships of domination in a given society is the appropriate starting point for ethics.

The reason they conclude this is both simple and instructive. A professor who announced a course on ethics without displaying familiarity with oppressor/oppressed relationships would be unable in Europe today to secure a student audience. The intellectual distance which separates North Americans from the rest of our western civilization is sharply revealed in this. As a gathering of intellectuals we are by comparison almost uniformly conservative, and in danger of being isolated in that conservatism.

Our own moral sensitivities are likely to be shaped by American pragmatism and its insistence upon immediate relevance. "Yes, but what's the practical thing to do?" is our typical response. We fail to observe that in this response is presupposed the established power relationships which already largely define what is viewed as practical or impractical. Against this Fourez urges the language of Utopia. By this he means not impotent dreaming but the task of envisioning a structural and systematic alternative to established and official "reality."

Our conscience in this country is often influenced by our historic ties to British Utilitarianism. We ask: "What is the greatest good for the greatest number?" This way of seeking the right is much like taking a vote or doing a consumer preference poll. What the majority *thinks* benefits the majority—that's what's right. But this way of reckoning what is morally to be preferred fails to grasp the function of ideology in society—its role of legitimating the interests of dominating groups, and co-opting other groups whose real interests remain veiled and confused.

That is why Fourez believes the task of ethics must begin with analyzing the established power relationships, laying bare a given society's inner institutional relationships and decoding its legitimating myths.

This debunking task is understood by religious ethicists in Europe and Latin America today, whether Protestants like Pannenberg and Metz or Catholics like Gutierrez or Fourez, as identical with the prophetic call "to break the idols" and hence a recovery of the ethical core of our western religious heritage. That theologians can be aided in this task by the instruction of Karl Marx seems to them an irony that is not at all unacceptable.

It is an irony which was last fully appreciated in this

country by Reinhold Niebuhr. In his *Moral Man and Immoral Society* (1932) Niebuhr brilliantly analyzed the class bias of conventional conscience. It is a bias which confuses propriety with morality, and while practicing minor virtues routinely enjoys the fruits of major (i.e. structural) vices. Niebuhr's debunking of moral pretension, in an age of frustrated ambition and anxious conformity much like our own, was withering. Fourez breathes this same air of iconoclasm. It is refreshing.

Why is it that Europe and Latin America speak more easily today for the prophetic heritage? Perhaps it is the same reason our own country spawned such powerful religious and social protests against voracious privilege in the first thirty years of this century. Then others were the world empires. We remained, economically, a kind of internally nourished giant. It was easier to see the sins of world avarice.

Now? It is we who bestride the world.

There is a second level of "strangeness" to Fourez for American readers. It involves what is to us the curious fact that he is an elementary particle physicist by training and profession, and also while continuing his scientific research instructs classes in ethics at a Technical Institute in Belgium, and remains throughout a practicing Catholic priest.

The division and specialization of knowledge realms is something which, as Max Weber has shown, is much easier for a broadly Protestant culture to live with than for a culture within which still lingers the memories of a medieval community of humanistic inquiry. There is in Fourez the spirit of Erasmus—the sense that all things human must finally be seen whole. Science, ethics, religion—these go their separate ways only to their mutual impoverishment. Fourez represents the best of Western intellectuality as he struggles to keep them in dialogue, each learning from the other.

Finally, there is in Fourez a remarkable gentleness which accompanies his insistent structural analysis. It is a quality that reveals itself especially in Part II, where he turns to interpersonal relations. He displays sensitivity and insight into such matters as human injury and repair, forgiveness and fidelity which we more often associate with novelists than theologians. It shows that Fourez is not a strident and brittle but a warm and compassionate person.

Indeed, the further one gets into this book the more one discovers that he or she is on a continuing voyage of reflection. We are surprised when, suddenly, whole new vistas open up. It's a book that will return well on the investment of a cover-to-cover reading.

John C. Raines
Department of Religion
Temple University

# PREFACE

This book intends to show that ethics is liberating only when people are aware of its cultural, political, and economic presuppositions, which necessarily stem from a specific place and time in history. Because every ethical endeavor should confess its societal conditions, I will begin by clarifying the context and the conditions of this book's production. It originated in a course on ethics I was giving to science students, and it bears some marks of its first audience. University students tend to see society from their own perspective, which is that of relatively privileged people. However, they also experience, as do most members of the middle class, powerlessness when they are confronted with the educational system or with the society in which they have to find a place.

This essay on ethics is not written from a neutral point of view. Although I intend to provide my readers with some analytical tools with which they will be able to decide for themselves, the essay is connected to a societal project that is partially determined by my personal choices and solidarities. To present these, it can be useful to mention my own evolution with respect to moral philosophy.

By my social origins, I was a part of the "open" Christian bourgeoisie. The ethics of that social class—its concern for persons and its way of giving to each individual a human value—influenced me. But at the same time I was influenced by its very individualistic approach. If the *other* was an important concern of mine, the *others*, as a collective group, was almost unknown to me. It was the same as far as systemic questions were concerned. Without being aware of it, I assumed the frames of reference of the establishment, which I confused with a universal order. Although I was a liberal in the Church, I did not notice how often the Church's positions are influenced by relationships between ecclesiastical structures and our society's conservative interests.

My change in attitude can be traced to several sources, starting with my temperament and also my education. I was open and ready to think differently from many people in my environment. My Christian education and my confrontation with the Gospel also brought me to the point where too-well-established patterns of thinking exploded. These influences also made me aware of Jesus's solidarity with the oppressed and the rejected, and that had an impact on my personal choices. Moreover, my training and my research work as an elementary particle physicist opened me to other realities by making me aware of a way of respecting facts that Christians (be they from the left or from the right) did not always share, as they tend to ideologize or to moralize. This research made me aware also of an environment that had nothing to do with the prejudices of the Christian bourgeoisie. Finally, as strange as it may seem to some, it was through statistical physics that I first met the collective aspect of human problems. Only later did I get acquainted with sociological, ideological, and institutional analysis, through which I became better able to understand the collective dimensions of a radical solidarity.

This evolution brought me to the point of choosing my solidarity with those who struggle on the side of the oppressed and the exploited, toward the promotion of societal structures that would eradicate the present causes of injustices. I practice that solidarity mainly through my intellectual work in a university, but also through involvement with some activist groups in the labor movement. These choices of mine have an impact on this essay on ethics.

It is from this point of view, then, that I now analyze the oppressions, the exploitations, and the sexism that underlie our choices. My hope (but hope can never be completely analyzed) is for another, growing, reality that can already be observed: the reality of possible liberations, of even partially realized liberations. Indeed, I believe that if so many yearn for liberation, it is because we already experience it in some aspects of our lives. Beyond the many kinds of master-slave relationships that exist, we also know the tenderness of human relationships. If that vision were to be lost, our analyses would produce only the darkness of a closed horizon. I recognize in history a positive growth, a hope that gives warmth to the most precise analyses. These partial liberations open our ethical choices to some intrusion of a meaning in history. But that intrusion can never be reduced to analysis; it always remains singular, gratuitous, and subsequent to the choices of those who commit themselves.

In this book, I present, through an analysis derived from my particular roots, one view of some possible meanings of human choices. But I leave to each his or her decisions. The function of ethics is not to moralize, but rather to outline critical thinking that indicates, from the outside, some possibilities for human decision and action. As Blondel stated it:

"La science de la pratique établit qu'on ne supplée pas à la pratique."[1] ("The science of decision-making finally shows that nothing can replace decision-making.") No analysis can ever completely explain the choices taken. Why do some take the less-traveled road? One never really knows.

The chapters of this book have been written so that they can for the most part be read separately. The first part (Chapters 1 – 5) examines the place of ethics in our society. It examines the way ethical codes are produced in a society and investigates the meaning of ethical norms. Chapter 6 provides a framework for a consideration of personal and relational ethics. Chapter 7 deals with questions related to the ethics of emotional and sexual life, and situates these questions in a broader societal context. The next three chapters are an introduction to systemic or structural ethics, which deals with the collective dimensions of human life. The last chapter considers a question very relevant to individuals facing an unjust society: where do activists or committed people find energy, élan, and courage to work toward the transformation of society?

1. Maurice Blondel, *L'Action* (1893) (Paris: Presses Universitaires de France, 1950), p. 463.

# ACKNOWLEDGMENTS

I want to thank all those who have helped me with their remarks, criticism, and suggestions: my students, my colleagues, and my friends. Among many, I want to mention: J. Baufay, J. Borremans, P. Ph. Druet, Ch. Ehlinger, J. M. Faux, Ch. Franck, C. Gortebecke, E. Herr, B. Hogan, P. de Locht, J. Raines, C. Robbs, G. Thill, P. Tihon. I want to thank Mr. David Morris, who wrote the first draft of the translation. I want to mention the secretarial help of J. Cratin, N. Renkin, and C. Robin; the support of my university in Belgium (Facultés Universitaires de Namur) and of La Salle College (Philadelphia); the concern of Mr. K. Arnold, Editor in Chief of Temple University Press, and of Mr. W. Day, Production Editor.

# PART ONE

# 1

# TABOOS, NORMS, VALUES

In this approach to ethics, I shall first consider a phenomenon important in all societies: the existence of norms or taboos. To find them, we need only to go as far as our immediate experience: *Thou shalt not kill, thou shalt not commit incest* are common taboos. *Thou shalt not covet thy neighbor's property, thou shalt respect authority, thou shalt honor thy father and thy mother* are examples of familiar norms.

By taboos and norms, I mean here those commands that might even be regarded as facts in our society. We don't know where they come from, but there they are, and it is unthinkable to oppose them. The source of their authority is not clear. They are older than any member of the society, and they underlie any individual decision. In our society today, most people do not like to speak about norms or taboos.

They prefer the word "value." This word gives the feeling (or the illusion) of allowing more freedom for the individual.

Taboos, norms, and values do not have the same meaning when they are offered in different places or by different people. For example, the meaning of the value "respect for authority" is quite different for persons who identify with the powerful than it is for those who submit to them, for a landowner and for his hired hand. The same is true of many other values, including that of "justice." The claim that justice is a value has quite different meanings according to whether it is pronounced by those who make the laws and fix employment contracts or by those who have no say in the matter. Examples like these are manifold, so that we see in the end that even those values that seem as "universal" as "respect for life" are not unequivocal in meaning. That is why we can only understand them if we refer to a broader theory, namely, that of ideologies.

### How are values legitimized?

Positivist sociology tends to speak of values as facts. It ignores the existence of dominating relationships, which could be at the root of any discourse that speaks of values, norms, or taboos. The theory of ideologies starts from a different point of view. It speaks of values, not as autonomous entities, but only with reference to what people say about human behavior within social relationships. Everything that people express in that context is called *ideological*. Ideological discourses are defined as social representations or images that *mobilize* groups and individuals, especially by giving them images of options that are possible for them. Furthermore, such representations or statements have a *legitimizing* role, because they link behavior to certain actions and stories that are looked upon as fundamental to the society. Finally, ideological stories or statements—through the way in which they interpret and legitimize events—*eliminate other possible interpretations and conceal the particular source of the criteria* that have been used. Thus, in a society built on relations of domination, the ideology often tends to conceal these relations.

Ideologies are often contrasted with science. However, there is no fundamental difference between an ideological language and a scientific one. In principle, scientific language is the one for which a frame of reference—what is called a paradigm—is relatively well determined, while ideological language characteristically uses ill-defined paradigms. Nevertheless, because in any discourse the frame of reference is always more or less ill-defined—merely conventional, if not arbitrary—all statements are ideological, even if they are called scientific. At the most extreme, one could even say that all language is ideological. It is, however, rather convenient to use the word "ideology" only to define those discourses whose criteria of reference are obviously ill-defined, so that one can say neither who enunciates them nor from what standpoint they are issued. This view of many discourses contrasts with that of those people who claim to be capable of making a radical distinction between scientific statements (objective and neutral) and ideological ones (subjective and biased).

Ideological statements do not all function in the same way. It is particularly useful to distinguish between ideology in its strictest form and Utopia. Ideology is a representation of the world as a whole within which we insert our fragmentary knowledge, thereby giving people roots within a universe. In this way it has a positive function, because it enables us to situate action and thereby to give it value. Ideology also contains some knowledge of the world, because it reflects what has been thought, and therefore mentally constructed, in a given society. But in general, ideology presents the point of view of the powerful in society while hiding real social relationships. It is therefore one representation of what *is*, an interpretation of the past. A Utopia, on the other hand, is a dream of what *might be*. It is also a picture, and thus a work of the imagination. By giving a background to action and giving an idea of what could be a "good" society, a Utopia fulfills an essential function for action. Neither ideology nor Utopia, however, is felt or thought about as such: both are a background to action; "they are a starting-point for thought rather than the subject of it."[1]

## Criticisms of ideologies: science and prophecy

Ideological discourses can be subjected to critical judgment. Peter Kemp makes a distinction between two ways of doing so: by scientific language and by mytho-poetic language.[2] Scientific language, although always full of ideological statements, can, if it unveils its criteria, produce partial fields of knowledge that challenge ideological images of the world. That is how some images and some Utopias can be denounced as unrealistic. However, since there is a constant link between the sciences and ideological statements, such criticisms are never final or complete. The economic sciences, for instance, can expose dominating relationships between countries, whereas the ideology of aid to developing countries conceals them; but the same economic sciences could in the name of "scientific realism" criticize some Utopias that are quite realizable. One could mention here the "scientific" arguments raised in the nineteenth century

1. Paul Ricœur, "Science et idéologie," *Revue Philosophique de Louvain,* May 1974, p. 333.

2. Cf. Peter Kemp, "L'Engagement dans le débat nucleaire, le probleme d'une ethique politique," symposium held in Namur, September 1977. The following pages are much inspired by that paper.

about social progress. The same is true of technologies. In the debate about nuclear power, for example, technical studies hide some ideological arguments as they show that some Utopias are scarcely possible. However, these scientific and technical statements are based on fragmentary knowledge. They may challenge ideologies, but they have no sounder basis themselves than the ideologies they challenge and they cannot replace the ideologies.

Mytho-poetic language, which includes the language of religion, is another type of ideological discourse that can be used to provoke critical judgment. This language characteristically presents an image or a myth concerning human existence. It is not a direct image of the world, nor is it linked to a given political stand, but it is concerned with both of these and is not usually clearly distinguishable from them. For example, statements about human brotherhood, original sin, the story of Jesus giving his life, liberty, and so forth, do not directly determine particular ideologies or Utopias, but they do raise questions and offer a picture or a poem which an ideological or utopian response will have to face up to. Furthermore, these images may act as a support and final recourse for criticism of policies that have become totalitarian and overpowering.

We have already seen ideological images in action. The myth of free enterprise is an ideological tale of liberal societies; in the same way, an analysis that starts by examining dominating relationships bears the marks of solidarity with the dominated groups. Since no language can be completely precise about its source, its standpoint, or the criteria it applies, it is always partly ideological. There is no completely neutral, precise, or objective statement. Our world is built by our ideological language and no one escapes this fact.

### Where do ideological statements stem from?

There is an important difference between discourses that support those in power and discourses that support the oppressed. Indeed, when the dominant groups of a society produce an ideology, one of its functions is to hide the dominant relationships. Consequently, a dominant group's ideological discourse would be undermined and useless if it highlighted the dominating relationships. Thus, when those in power pronounce an ideological statement, one only has to ask what criteria were used for the statement to discredit the statement to some degree. When, for example, it is taken for granted that men should give the orders in a male-dominated society, one has only to ask a question about the underlying criteria for that assumption to lose its impact.

Similarly, stressing freedom rather than proscriptions in our industrialized societies is part of an ideology that supports the dominant groups by concealing social domination. That ideology loses much of its force as soon as social constraints are revealed, and the vast range of proscriptions becomes obvious. In other words, to keep their privileges, the dominant groups have to use ideologies that legitimize and conceal the dominating relationships. For the oppressed groups, on the other hand, there is no point in concealing the existence of these relationships. Therefore the ideology, taken in a much more restricted sense than before, appears as the language of the dominant groups (or those who support them), concealing its criteria in order to conceal the dominating relationship.

A very simple example will make this quite clear. If someone describes a situation in which one person is treading on the foot of another and I hear it said that the two feet are in a symmetrical position, one on top of the other and in an exactly equivalent situation, I know very well that I am listening to the person who is doing the treading. If, on the other hand, the one whose foot is being squashed is speaking, he will not speak about the position of the two feet as symmetrical, but rather he will say he is being trodden upon. In this sense, the ideological version par excellence is the interpretation of the master or of someone on the master's side. On the contrary, the slave's version would not be ideological, insofar as the slave at least does not have the same interest in concealing the dominating relationships.

### Dominating relationships

We can make the above statements even clearer if we go into what we mean by the concepts "dominating relationships" or "oppressor-oppressed relationships." These are theoretical concepts for the sake of analysis, that is, they make it possible to understand situations while remaining always dependent on interpretations. Thus, if we look at Belgium in 1944 or Vietnam in 1970, the concept of "war" can be useful for understanding what was going on. The same is true for the concept of "dominating relationships." Such a concept, however, also has its limits: speaking of dominant relationships does not mean that one can always pick out individuals as being dominated or dominant. Everyone is one or the other at different times. Similarly, some social groups (such as the middle class) can be both oppressor and oppressed. But these concepts, used as intellectual categories, make it possible to typify those relationships in which some people have some non-reciprocated power over others. To understand this theoretical category, the parable of the master and the slaves may be useful.

The master is the one who, in a past conflict with the slaves, forced the slaves to fear for their existence to such an extent that, in the end, they gave up their freedom to the master. The slaves lost everything except their lives, while the master gained privileges and a special condition. Consequently, the master and the slaves are in contrary situations. The slaves depend on the master for their security; they are dominated. The masters, by contrast, in order to safeguard their position, must defend their advantages with the danger of becoming alienated by using all their energy to fight for the privileges they must protect. What masters and slaves have to say about this situation will be quite different, depending on the extent to which they have to or want to cooperate with each other in order to produce what is necessary for their existence. Indeed, the masters must hide from the slaves the possibility that they, the slaves, might revolt; it is therefore extremely important to the masters to have an ideology that conceals the dominant relationship binding them. The slaves, for their part, have less to lose from seeing this relationship. That is why, when one uses the restricted sense of the word, ideological language is always the masters discourse; it motivates those they dominate, justifies their privileges, and hides the reality of the dominating relationship. That, moreover, is why the master's speech shows little evidence of a sense of humor. The slaves, however, have less to hide and may even laugh at everything. Nevertheless, it may also happen that the slaves will want to have the illusion of being masters; in that case, the slaves will also conceal the dominating relationships and borrow the masters language; we already mentioned how this leads to what we shall call "ideological domination."

Many examples of ideological discourse—in this restricted sense of the master's language—could be given: the way men justify and hide the man/woman dominating relationship, the way owners and employers try to mask the dominating relationship underlying the concept of private property, the way doctors defend their profession, and so forth.

Reluctance to clarify the criteria used reveals the ideological nature of a statement. Let us take an example. The statement: "Our students are much appreciated" is obviously completely ideological. In reality, the students are only appreciated in relation to certain criteria and by specific persons or groups. The only people who profit by hiding these criteria are those who have an interest to defend. The faculty, for example, will benefit from saying that the students are much appreciated, without saying by whom or according to what criteria, but just in a universal kind of way. Trade union representatives, on the other hand, will perhaps have a vested interest in saying that the students are only appreciated in relation to certain well-defined criteria and that, for example, they have a bad record as far as solidarity with the working class is concerned. One could perhaps even set up the methodological principle that the more privileges people have to defend, the more what they say must conceal the situation; and, on the other hand, the less people have to defend, the less embarrassed they are to define precisely the criteria underlying what they say.

Later on we shall examine how ideologies are produced, what their links are with political and economic institutions, and how they help to provide a society with ethical and moral codes. However, we must first look in greater detail at another phenomenon: the internalization of the ideology.

### The prisons in which the prisoners are the wardens

There is a familiar phenomenon in which those who apparently have the least interest in supporting a particular ideology are often those who actually propagate it the most. For example, many women consider it natural to be submissive and dominated. The most typical example, however, is probably that of the old servants at the manor, who were even more ready than their masters to affirm their lack of rights. This is a clear case of the mechanism called ideological domination: people are so conditioned by an ideology that they become accomplices to the oppressive relationships that dominate them. The servants in the manor have accepted the ideology so wholeheartedly that it no longer requires any force to maintain the domination that the ideology gives over them. At this stage, domination no longer uses brutal repression; it is the stage of ideological domination. A situation exists in which the dominated persons have a self-image that makes it impossible for them to get out of this state. An alternative image, one of non-domination, cannot be imagined.

Obviously, this is the state of affairs that the dominant group and those who share its interests seek. The dominated people often (even unconsciously) play their game because they also get an advantage out of it: physical and mental security. Inasmuch as they accept and legitimize their own oppression, they have less to fear from their masters, who need no longer bring them to heel. The gentleness of the oppressed ones and their gentle tactics correspond to this desire for security. One thinks of the traditional picture of the woman, for example. Insofar as the domination is completely ideological, it is impossible for the dominated to modify anything.

The opposite process, by which ideological domination becomes direct domination, is called "conscientization," or the process of becoming aware. This process unveils the ideological language that concealed the domination and made it almost "natural," so that the relative strength of both parties is revealed. Just as ideological domination creates a feeling of security, growing awareness creates anxiety. This explains why dominated people often show resistance to awareness. Many women or workers, for example, prefer not to see the relations of domination that affect them as women or as workers; they are more at ease in the present social role than in the insecurity of change. This is all the more so since dominant ideologies portray certain aspects of servitude as values; for example, think of certain characteristics attributed to femininity.

It does not take great learning to realize that, quite often, ethical language and moral codes play a role in ideological domination. One has only to read Napoleon's *Imperial catechism*, which gives the moral attitudes to adopt in front of the civil authorities, to notice that the function of that section of that catechism is to assert the emperor's domination. In that case, the ideological practice is so flagrant that almost anyone can notice it. This is not always the case, however. For instance, it is sometimes difficult to see whether some "values" promote the interests of the dominant groups or, quite the contrary, foster a certain liberation from dominating relationships. If, for example, one considers some codes or family morals, their links with economic, political, and cultural domination are not always obvious. It is, consequently, not unusual for some ethical statements that at first sight seem quite harmless to turn out also to be ideological, reinforcing a particular type of established "order" or, rather, "disorder."

Finally, let us note that the oppressed often add to their ideological domination by imagining the world and society in an oversimplified way, rather than according to existing strength ratios. Their status, which deprives them of critical knowledge, often leads them to believe that revolutionary changes will be easy. As a result, when they fail they become even more helpless and more dominated.

### Internalized self-censorship and guilt feelings

The internalization of ideological domination is not the most powerful form of internalization. People who own nothing can listen to or make statements legitimizing the private ownership of the means of production without realizing their full significance; but if those people were made more aware of things, they could be motivated to dismantle the structure. Ideological statements are part of a rational framework that legitimizes certain situations. A more profound internalization takes place in what psychoanalysis calls the superego and the process of *repression*.

In this process, societal proscriptions are identified with the most ancient of our psychological censorships, which psychoanalysis considers to be linked with the Oedipus conflict and the "father's rule." Proscriptions internalized in this way are so profoundly attached to people's psychology that they are often called the "inner voice of conscience." Such internalization has an important social function. As examples, let us consider respect for property, and adultery. Laws and moral codes that encourage respect for property or forbid adultery can in themselves be very effective tools in the management of society. But social control is even more complete when the society's individuals have internalized these laws to the extent that, at the very moment when they would like to infringe on them, an inner voice tells them firmly and with authority: "Don't do that." That is the censorship role of the superego; like a taboo, it forbids any action that infringes on the internalized moral codes. One can thus realize the important social role fulfilled by what is often called the "formation of conscience." This contribution is not to be considered only in negative terms. On certain occasions we are very happy to have some internalized social orders. This is the case, for example, when that inner voice prevents us from killing someone while we are angry.

Psychoanalysis and other psychotherapeutic practices are intended to help people free themselves from these commands that act on the subconscious; the goal of these therapies is to enable people to decide for themselves how to face the ideologies and the conflicts they are involved in. To this extent psychoanalysis is less of a cure, in the sense that doctors cure someone who is ill, than it is a way of giving the person enough control over unconscious processes to be able to manage them.

The internalization of norms from parents and society is the basis of guilt feelings. These are the feelings that we have when something inside us reproaches us without our being able to identify its source. Psychologists call the cause of these feelings the *superego*. To use a term borrowed from transactional analysis, on could say that the guilty person feels that he or she is in front of an angry parent who is scolding him. This feeling is different from shame, which is the feeling of being unworthy to have one's place in the sun or the desire to disappear, without necessarily facing an "angry parent." It is also different from regret, in which one considers that if the same circumstances were to occur again, one would act differently.

Guilt stems not from an "objective" value accorded to one's achievements, but rather from internalized norms. Individuals and groups can decide that some norms are usefully internalized and others are not. Thus, I consider profitable the internalization of a norm that forbids me to kill another person and that would arouse a feeling of guilt in me if I wished to do so in my anger. One can understand, however, that a person would consider inappropriate a norm that engendered feelings of guilt concerning all sexual behavior.

We can therefore consider guilt as an alarm signal put in place by society, through education, that automatically warns individuals when they infringe on internalized norms. Some of these signals are beneficial, others are not. In any case, it is scarcely healthy to remain at the level of unconscious guilt. The feeling of guilt, which owes its strength to a "program" recorded during one's formative experiences, frees some psychic energy for use in the immediate situation.

If that psychic energy remains backward-looking, the feeling becomes a *complex*: the individual reacts to situations by repeating behavior or sticking to the psychological program that sufficed before, without undertaking actions suited to the immediate situation. Guilt can also be reinforced by irritation with oneself in a self-punishing process called remorse. This usually does not help, although it may sometimes provoke an appropriate and responsible decision.

Finally, many people are unable to get rid of a guilt feeling that seems inappropriate because they go about it the wrong way. They become angry with themselves for having guilt, with the result that they become doubly irritated as the feeling of guilt is multiplied by their anger at it. They then often feel like a child facing two angry, conflicting adults: completely paralyzed! To move beyond such a feeling, the best procedure to follow is usually more or less the same as that used by an educator to help such a paralyzed child. Scolding the child and telling him that he shouldn't be paralyzed only aggravates the situation. But if the child is given confidence, if he feels understood and is smiled at kindly, he will take heart and strength. Similarly, if we treat ourselves with understanding when we feel inappropriate guilt, realizing that that feeling is the result of our past, and if we love ourselves despite that limitation, the inappropriate feeling will gradually be totally or partially "disinternalized." For deeply rooted guilt feelings, however, years of treatment may be needed.

Our attitude toward people in authority (often called father images in Freudian terminology) is a key one among our important internalizations. Every individual must, in one way or another, discover how to behave in relation to people in authority. As children we have to obey, and the way we react later as adults will depend on our development. People who continue to feel dominated may become obedient,

sometimes even servile, adults. There may also be the opposite response of reacting against any father figure, leading
to a life of perpetual rebellion. This attitude of permanent revolt may seem irrational. Psychoanalysts say that it reflects
the internal struggle of someone trying to be himself in the
face of authority. Deep inside even the obedient or servile
adult, there may be the rumblings of the repressed (but sometimes near the surface) desire to "kill the father." (This obviously does not necessarily refer to a physical murder or to
the murder of the father "begetter"; the term is symbolic.)

Finally, a happy solution to this problem is often found
by saying that someone has managed to become the "friend
of the father." This means that henceforth the person can be
on equal terms with figures of authority: neither obsequious
nor automatically rebellious.

### Choosing a social standpoint

Ethics is a kind of ideological discourse. It is always
linked to the social position of those who are presenting it. It
is thus important to clarify our starting point for describing
human actions. Our point of departure has been the existence of taboos and norms in human society. This choice
was, to a certain extent, an arbitrary one. After all, every description of human behavior does not necessarily begin by
stating that there are prohibitions. Other people may start
from a different viewpoint, such as that of individual freedom and of their ability to achieve whatever they wish. In
other words, there is always a choice in the way of explain-
ing or interpreting human behavior.

I do not think that such a choice can be rationally justified, because it relates to the very framework that defines
the rationality within which one's analysis of the history of
humankind is carried out. This simply means that our "read-

ing" always takes place in history, in a specific place and from a particular social standpoint. The choice I have made here favors the recognition of moral mechanisms, norms, and domination, rather than the uncritical affirmation of the freedom of individuals. Although this decision cannot be completely justified on a rational basis, its context can be shown. Who sees individuals in a society as being free and feels free himself? Who, on the other hand, sees people as being subject to proscriptions? Those people in a society who are in power, who are dominant, the ruling classes, see first of all the possibility of action, freedom. Those, however, who are members of dominated groups, or who see the world from the point of view of the powerless and are sympathetic to them, are much more aware, from the start, of the limits and norms imposed on their actions. We shall see later that the middle classes usually identify themselves with the dominant groups and call themselves free, but their liberty is usually limited to the psychological realm. I believe, therefore, that the choice of recognizing the prohibitions on, rather than extolling the freedom of, humankind is part of a vision of the world seen in solidarity with dominated groups.

### The myth of free enterprise or the myth of original sin?

To understand our perspective, it would be useful to consider the views arising from the opposite perspective: that of the myth of free enterprise.[3] When people using this myth as a frame of reference look at human behavior, they start by talking about freedom and the wide range of possibilities open to individuals. They do not speak, for exam-

3. In this context, I use the word "myth" in a very broad sense: the image or story to be found underlying a concept of the world. It is a world view or a story that makes it possible to "read" or "interpret" what is happening.

ple, about liberation, that is, the process of moving from domination toward a greater freedom. On the contrary, they stress their belief that everybody actually is free and perhaps equal.

Underlying this myth we find the theme that everything is possible for everybody. It is easy to see that this description of the world cannot come from slaves, but only from masters, from those for whom, if not every action is possible, at least many are. At the root of this ethics, which we shall call the dominant ethics, and which stems from the myth of free enterprise, there seems to be the world view of those who "own" society and who have privileges. This perspective supposes that all individuals can achieve their aims in life without any changes in society. It believes that history does not affect individuals and that everyone is equal at birth. Human beings can fulfill their destinies by using their own initiative, by pulling themselves up by their bootstraps. They are entirely responsible for their own success and therefore guilty of their own failures. In general, moreover, a certain conception of tolerance and non-confrontation completes this description of the world. All this can be looked upon as the "civil religion" of America.

This vision is quite different from the one that starts by noting the taboos, domination, and limitations that most people experience in their lives. According to this point of view, which can be described as the myth of original sin, the world is not considered *a priori* as "the best of all worlds" (that is, the world as seen by those who organize it), but as a world that bears its historical burden.[4] To understand this point of view, which seems to us to be related to the experiences of

4. When, in this book, I speak of the "myth of original sin," obviously, I do not cover all classical theological doctrine on the subject. Obviously also I do not mean the decadent form of the myth, which supposes that original sin is like a spot on the child's soul.

the dominated classes, one could perhaps simply look at what Christian theology has called original sin.

This doctrine supposes that, by the very fact of being a member of human society as it has historically developed, every individual feels limitations and is partly paralyzed by them. It recognizes that human relations are what Christian theology has called relationships of sin, that is, relationships in which people do not consider each other as equals or as loving, but in which people mutually oppress one another. It also believes that injustice and oppression are not automatic phenomena, but are linked to human history. History thus imposes a limit on freedom that, according to the myth of free enterprise, was given to humanity "by nature." Everyone has their place and role in a community of sin or a community of oppression. This contrasts with the individualism of the dominant groups, which considers people to be so unconnected that the actions of one person are assumed to leave other people untouched. Everyone is an accomplice and a part of the relations of oppression, and nobody escapes the consequences of oppression; but nobody is personally responsible for this collective situation.

Furthermore, according to this "original sin" myth, one cannot speak of individual liberation or salvation. Rather, there is no salvation outside a liberating community, and salvation will never be complete until, at the end of time, the Kingdom of God has destroyed the burden of domination caused by human history. Here again we see how different this view is from that which supposes that everyone, alone, by their own individual efforts, finds salvation and liberation. Finally, in this picture of the world built around the myth of original sin, conflict is considered a normal part of existence; this is very far from the liberal doctrine of tolerance, where the ideal is to avoid arguments. The myth, by manifesting historical oppression in the world, calls for historical movements of liberation.

The description I have just presented as a starting point for a study of human behavior keeps its distance from the paradigm that largely characterizes American sociology.[5] The presupposition of equality, characteristic of this type of sociology, is to be found in those ideologies that, in one way or another, preserve "the world" as the dominant ideologies describe it. In contrast, I have considered from the very start the proscriptions and relations of dominance. I have not supposed that descriptions of the world could be neutral, nonhistorical, permanent. Rather, I took into consideration that history does not leave individuals in equivalent situations with respect to each other and to their actions.

This point of view is that of the Christian doctrine of original sin, but it is also Marx's point of view when he recognizes that the historical development of the means of production has placed us in the middle of a class struggle. It is also Freud's when, in his own way, he disputes the more or less moralizing and voluntarist theories of psychology, and re-places individuals in their own stories or contexts, to see how their family situation and the societal norms they internalized within their superegos form the basis of their analysis. Underlying the frame of reference in all these approaches is the choice of a category, which illustrates the relationships of dominance, and which calls for liberation.

The objection that may be raised to what I have said above hinges on the acknowledgment of proscriptions, because in modern descriptions of human behavior it is not fashionable to mention them. Instead, it is considered better today to present things in a more positive light and to speak of values.

5. This paradigm shows uncritical acceptance of an initial, empirical "reading" of society, in the name of a certain objectivity. Such categories as "domination" are often rejected as being too "subjective."

### Proscriptions or values?

Values, as sociology, especially the American positivist school, defines them, are those forms of conduct that members of a society consider acceptable and desirable. According to a number of moralists, the language of proscriptions should be abandoned in favor of the proposal of values to individuals and groups as well as to whole societies.

It seems to me that such an attitude is full of ambiguities. Why do people insist on offering values and moral norms in a positive light when in society itself they appear primarily in the form of taboos and proscriptions? What is it really all about? Is it a matter of sugaring the pill, or of really changing the dominating mechanisms that are expressed in the system of proscriptions? I do not feel that it is necessary to make a detailed study of society to become convinced that, even under a more positive light, the proscriptions are still there. Those who do not accept the norms of our Western, free-enterprise society are pitilessly rejected, even if it is done in the name of "values" rather than of taboos. The changeover from an ethic of proscriptions to one of values partly corresponds, perhaps, to a desire not to recognize the reality of relations of domination at work in society.

It may be helpful to look at a corresponding development in certain structures of modern corporate management. Whereas previously management was seen to be authoritarian and tough, nowadays the hardness is carefully disguised. Sometimes people who have been fired almost feel obliged to thank the manager who told them to leave, so "humanely" was it done. Indeed, managers scarcely speak of people being fired any more; rather, we hear of persons "losing their job" and "being thanked for their services." There is a characteristic trend behind a whole technology of management intended to camouflage the dominating relationship. This is not entirely a bad thing, since, as long as one isn't being fired, it is pleasant to be treated as if an implacable authority did not exist at a higher level, and as if one had complete freedom of initiative. As long as a person is at one with the company, this situation is rather nice. As soon as that feeling of solidarity ends, however, and the real lines of power between employer and employee appear, then things are quite different.

The shift from morals of proscriptions to morals of values hides the same kind of situation. As long as individuals feel more or less in collaboration with the society that offers them certain "values," this way of presenting ethics gives a very pleasant illusion of freedom and conceals the toughness that is camouflaged behind these "values." However, as soon as the individual, for whatever reason, feels less solidarity with the hidden powers that determine these "values," that person quickly uncovers the prohibitions that a liberal society puts under the superficial covering of tolerance and that do not look very different from those of any other society. Consequently, the ideological shift that turns morals of proscriptions into morals of values has perhaps closer links than one suspects with a managerial, individualistic society.

In any case, it is more pleasant for members of the privileged groups in society to hear of values being "offered" than it is to come face to face with the naked force relationships at work in society, which are usually associated with prohibitions. Thus, proscriptions are hardly mentioned in a liberal society, at least among its privileged groups; it is the supposedly chosen "values" that condition individual behavior. Our conditioning by values and by ethics is not so easy to unmask; it is, indeed, well concealed by the ideological discourse.

## 2

# WHERE DO MORAL CODES
# COME FROM?

Every society has its moral codes and its taboos. In most
cases, however, we do not know where they come from or
who lays them down, although in our society we are beginning to be aware of and to ask questions about their origins.
First we shall look at a kind of answer to these questions,
which I shall call *idealistic*, and which can be found in several different manifestations. Then we shall look at another
approach to the problem, which I shall call *historical*, and
which is typified by the fact that, in my opinion at least, it
pays greater attention to the historical origins of proscriptions than does the idealistic approach. The idealistic answer to the question, "Where do taboos and moral codes
come from?" will turn out to be strongly ideological, concealing its criteria and hiding societal conflicts as well as the
balance of power within society.

## The different types of idealistic answers

Historically, the existence of taboos has often been attributed directly to God. In some religions, God is the one who gives the commandments and says what may and may not be done. Seen in this light, it is clear who imposes the proscriptions: God. Such a position situates the production of taboos and moral codes elsewhere than in history, thus hiding their human and historical origins.

Taboos and moral codes have also often been discussed in a way that calls upon "human nature": the imposition of proscriptions springs from the nature of humanity and things. The attachment of importance to "nature" has its origins in a desire to maintain distance from the religious codes, which were usually imposed by the Church. Hence, people in the eighteenth and nineteenth centuries considered that no proscription or moral code could really be accepted unless it arose from "nature," which was taken to mean an impersonal standard that no person called his own and that applied to everyone. The Declaration of Independence makes this explicit in the beginning. It starts, not by stating a certain number of religious standards, but by stating that each man has a number of inalienable rights. These natural rights had the advantage of not depending on any of the diverse religious denominations; God is mentioned only as the one who decrees these natural rights. This reliance on nature meant, in fact, some emancipation from religion. However, what is often represented as human nature is usually just the idea the dominant classes of a society hold about its members. It is amusing to note, for example, that in a bourgeois democracy, everything that is considered human nature happens to resemble what the bourgeoisie considers to be virtuous.

In our technological society, there is a scientific ideology related to this nature ideology. It claims to be able to examine nature dispassionately and disinterestedly, and thus to be able to lay the foundations of morality "naturally."

Theories that try to base morality on "human finality" are a variation on those described above. They consider that humanity has—through divine decree or through its very nature—its own purpose. Moreover, anyone not working for this purpose will, in general, be considered as doomed to unhappiness. The way morality works in these theories is quite simple: anything helping forward the purpose of humanity is good; anything acting against it is bad. Those who believe they know this purpose find it possible to determine, by a simple rational process of fitting a means to an end, what is morally good. Such an approach does, however, have serious drawbacks, because, on close examination, one realizes that, as with "human nature," "human finality" is defined culturally. Whatever is proposed as the "purpose of humanity" can be shown to be a reflection of particular dominant ideologies. The same could be said of utilitarian ethics: what criteria are used to determine what is useful?

Finally, some people claim that proscriptions originate in the conscience: there is assumed to be, in everyone's heart, a voice that tells us what is right and what is wrong. For some, the voice of conscience is supposed to give precise orders. For others, it only gives general guidance, as, for example, to respect other people, to do what is good, to obey reason, and so forth. . . . In both cases, taboos come from the conscience. Nevertheless, only a little observation reveals that the individual conscience—the psychologists' "superego"—is only what education has made it in a given culture and society. The fact that human beings wonder about the meaning of their actions has, perhaps, deeper significance than any precise orders that emanate from consciences.[1]

1. Cf. the section of Chapter 5 entitled "The ethical dimension as a form and not as a norm."

### Idealism

Whether moral codes come from some human finality determined by God or by human nature, or are the product of individual consciences, or can be discovered through some analysis concerning utility, the structures of these theories are very similar. In each case, the possibility of talking about humanity in general is implicitly or explicitly presupposed. In other words, it is implied that one can determine moral codes with reference to a particular *idea* about humanity. This means that ideas about men and women, about the family, about property, about society, or about sexuality will determine the way in which moral codes are worked out. It is presupposed that, in one way or another, it is relevant to speak of humanity as a general concept, and that this more or less normative concept has a meaning in itself. According to these views, if we know what a human being is, we can determine how he or she should act. Indeed, this is the source of many humanistic doctrines based on "human dignity," "human rights," and so forth. In some cases, it is considered possible to define this *idea* of a human being *a priori*; in other cases, it is by studying the way humans act and think that one hopes to determine scientifically some conditions of their actions, and thus discover some of their general properties, *a posteriori*.

When speaking of idealism, one often refers to Plato. Broadly speaking, one can say that, in Plato's opinion, ideas come first; concrete realities are only the fruit of these ideas. Thus, human beings are only so many realizations of the perfect idea of humanity. Similarly, the squares that one sees are, according to Plato, the concrete materialization of the perfect idea of the square. The same is true for love, friendship, liberty, and so forth. If, for example, one speaks of love in an idealistic way, one will be referring—at least implicitly—to the idea of perfect, true love. Indeed, everyday language shows how often we are idealistic: we say, for example, that such and such a love isn't *really* love. In this way, we show that we refer to a certain normative idea of what love should be. Plato expressed this in his famous parable of the cave, in which he says that human beings in the world are like prisoners in a cave. Behind them there is a great fire, and in front of them stands a wall that acts more or less as a screen. Between the fire and the prisoners, but unseen by the prisoners, people pass along carrying vases, tools, and other objects. The prisoners never see anything but the shadows of the objects, and, since that is all they ever see, the shadows seem to be real objects. In their own world, they mistake the shadows for reality. But the real objects are the ones that cast the shadows.

Plato compares the world with that cave: the real world is the world of ideas, and what we see are only more or less deformed shadows and manifestations. Thus, there is an idea of a human being and then there are the human beings themselves, which are only reflections of the idea. Insofar as they desire to be perfect, people must match the idea as closely as possible. In this way we have a standard by which to determine normal human activity. Some people, for example, talk about *authentic human sexuality*; obviously, the more people behave according to the norms deduced from this idea, the more perfect they will be. Similarly, if an idea is formed once and for all of what the human family is, a whole series of norms can be deduced about how families ought to live. If there is an idea of femininity, it will be possible to work out how women ought to behave. Such principles can also be applied to social questions, such as politics and the state; based on an idea of the perfect society, one can work out how societies should be organized.

The answers I give in the preceding section to the question, "Where do moral codes come from?" all presuppose a final determination of what a human being, human nature, and human conscience are. According to one's point of view, these determinations are made by God, the nature of things, social utility, or a spiritual principle. In the long run, however, they all mean more or less the same thing: the normative, directive ideas about humanity have been given once and for all. It is on the basis of ideas such as these that moral codes have to be founded.

In this line of thought, however, it is important to stress the difficulty of defining the "authentic nature of things." In the case of sexuality, for example, long studies in philosophy, biology, psychology, sociology, and elsewhere are required to determine what sexuality is and to deduce codes of sexual morality. The same is true for human freedom, friendship, love, and so on. An idealistic approach, therefore, does not consist of doing without empirical study, but rather presupposes that it is meaningful and useful to search for universal answers to such general questions as: "What is a human being?" "What is a family?" "What is useful, now, in this society?" Furthermore, it assumes in general that the universal answers to such questions can be valid for all periods of history. This does not mean that people claim the ability to discover the final answer to what a human being is, or what a family is; but it is believed that eternally valid answers do exist. We should point out that this way of thinking is, moreover, linked to the non-historical perspective in which science often works. For example, it is thought that the concept of the atom has been determined once and for all in history and that it will never be modified. This does not mean that the theory of the atom will not be abandoned, but, at least from a methodological point of view, physicists presuppose that there is a right answer, which is the aim of any research activity in physics. In the same way, idealism in philosophy presupposes, at least as a governing principle, an answer to the questions that we have presented.

In an idealistic perspective, it is not considered necessary, when speaking of people, to mention the material and historical circumstances in which they find themselves today. It is considered possible to use a generic concept of humanity. If we refuse to talk about humanity in general, however, we do not imply that we feel unable to say anything about people and their constraints. A whole series of physical, biological, economic, political, cultural, and other limits exist and can be described. It is therefore possible, and meaningful, to determine what those limits and constraints are today. In this sense, concepts, such as human sexuality, for example, are useful constructs. However, refusing to be idealistic means not giving a once-and-for-all meaning to such ideas as human being, family, property, love, sexuality, and so on. It means recognizing that any discourse referring to these realities stems from a particular point of view. It seems to me impossible to prove that idealism is false or to show that there are no established ideas or blueprints in accordance with which human beings exist. However, by examining more closely the concrete notions that we use when speaking about men, women, sexuality, and so on, we realize that they do not come from eternal truths, as idealism would have us believe. On the contrary, they have their own particular place and origin in social history.

### Where do ideas come from?

Notions do not arise from just anywhere; our notions of the world always come from particular sources. In order to see how, let us consider how society works. It is interesting, for example, to notice that when, in a given culture, people talk in general terms about women or about femininity, their views take on the biases of a given society. Hence, in our Western society, people describe the life of women within our patriarchal culture. Are they then talking about a univer-

sal and eternal idea, or rather about the particular conceptions that our culture conveys about women?

To be even more specific, it should be added that it does
not make much sense to attempt to present the general view
about women in any society as a whole; it is more relevant
to see how the idea of women and femininity is understood
by *particular* groups *within* a given culture. Thus, in our
Western society, when people speak about femininity, they
usually think about the way women are considered in the
middle-class world. What is often presented as an eternal
idea of femininity is therefore in fact the ideological pro-
jection by certain groups or social classes of their own particular point of view. In the case of Western society, the most
widespread point of view has women "in their place," in
other words, dominated by men. If we examine the concept
of masculinity in the same way, similar results appear. Here
again, what is presented as an eternal idea of man is only the
reflection of what the dominant groups in society think
about men.

These analyses challenge the theory of eternal ideas
and, as a consequence, their use to morality. Thus, when certain present-day moralists talk about the eternal idea of the
family, it is droll to note that—quite by chance!—that idea
conforms to the dominant idea of the family in our society.
The same is true in regard to such concepts as private property, individual responsibility, love, and many others. In
every case, idealistic moralists present as an eternal idea
something that can be shown, under more critical scrutiny, to
be the historical product of a particular culture, or, more precisely, of a particular subculture. In extreme cases, when
people accept eternal ideas, they are not so far from the attitude of those who judged the "noble savages" according to
the criteria of our Western culture. Of course, all this leads us
to question any possible use of general ideas when they are

presented as universal and eternal. Is it possible to present an idea, a concept, or a norm that is not the product of a particular culture, and, more particularly, the product of groups that produced them? What meaning is there, then, in such notions as "true love" or "real friendship"?

To put it briefly, I question universal ideals, which are referred to as either explicit or implicit norms. All ideas that are presented as eternal need analysis to see how they rely on the dominant ideologies of a particular society. It is important to examine how ideologies that speak about love, friendship, responsibility, masculinity or femininity, family, private property, and so on, in fact underlie and legitimize the activities of the dominant groups. What is more, they generally hide the way in which domination is exerted.

### Dominant ideologies and dominant groups

We have seen that notions and norms come from somewhere; they reflect the power relations within a society. However, although the above analysis can be considered valid, it is also often ill-understood. Some people think that the dominant groups impose moral standards out of cynicism or self-interest, as if, for example, it was after a conscious decision that the nineteenth-century bourgeoisie extolled the virtues of private property. Such interpretations are not always wrong; some people have been known to encourage ethical education while saying that they didn't believe in it, but that it was useful . . . for keeping the people quiet. But in most cases, the power that imposes moral laws is diffused through all society and is more restrictive than it appears. In fact, it is not unusual—and this was the case for the nineteenth-century bourgeoisie as far as sexuality was concerned—for some privileged classes to find themselves the most restricted by ethical codes.

Indeed, ethical codes seem to be the result of a multitude of localized strategies that, little by little, give rise to ethical structures linked to a given society. For example, we will see later how the calculating ethics of the bourgeois merchants led them to control passions, and thus to build the puritan sexual ethic. The power that imposes these standards is not to be compared with a master planner lucidly and cynically directing everything, but rather with those multiple forces that cause gas molecules to expand uniformly within a vessel. There is not, of course, one dominant class that assumes sovereignty over ethical standards; the dominant groups are themselves part of a whole set of economic, political, and ideological forces, which they certainly help to consolidate and, perhaps, to create. However, the structure of ethical systems can usually be seen to reflect faithfully the entire social structure. That is how liberal, industrial society produces an ethic about private property.

The ethical ideas and systems espouse the interests of the socially dominant, but the mechanisms by which this happens are not so apparent or simple. Sometimes they come to the surface, as, for example, in parliamentary speeches in the last century, when obligatory school attendance was defended on the grounds that it would teach future factory workers punctuality. But in most cases, these mechanisms are so complex that only the final result can be seen. The multiple and diffused forces at work in the social field have produced results independent of the desires of individuals. Moreover, in many cases it is precisely in trying to avoid certain effects that the effects are produced. Very often the issues at stake are not those that, in all good faith, social actors intended to promote. In those cases some speak about the tricks of history. That does not mean that history is a tricky manipulator, but that there are diffused structures and mechanisms that produce definite and sometimes unexpected effects. Let us, for example, think about what encourages our contemporaries to accept the precept "Thou shalt seek ful-fillment." This precept is only one mechanism of social con-trol of a society that manipulates people by commanding them to be successful; the success of the individual has be-come the instrument of control. By a "trick" of history, the search for personal fulfillment has become a controlling so-cial device.

**3**

# THE PRODUCTION
# OF NOTIONS

One of the most important elements in Marx's contribution to the study of society was his suggestion that the world is not guided by ideas but, quite the contrary, that ideas are, at least up to a certain point, the results and the reflection of political and economic changes in our culture.[1]

## Economics and politics

Marx situates at the base of social life those organizations that produce what is necessary for survival: shelter, food, clothing, and other indispensable items. For Marx, the

1. It is precisely this "to a certain point" that Stalin's version of orthodox Marxism plays on, intending to suppress the independence of political and ideological institutions, thus laying the ideological foundations of totalitarianism.

way of producing determines the social structures. This does not mean that human life can be reduced to this economic level, but that, in the end, any society will have to accord importance to the production of what is essential to survival. But this does not deny the relative autonomy of other levels, such as the political or ideological levels.

Many social types of production are possible and have been used, depending on the available production techniques. There is, for example, a great difference between a self-sufficient medieval farm and the complex systems of the industrial world. A given type of production implies specific relations among producers; these are called production relations. Thus, the production relations in the medieval farm were very different from those found between employer and employee in a twentieth-century company. The type of production, therefore, introduces differences of roles, of power, of privileges, of rights, and so on, and thus determines social relations. These relations create the societal organization that is the basis of every political life. This organization in particular determines social classes, that is to say, groups characterized by their interests and created by production relations and types of production. These class interests are determined, not by individual desires, but by the roles linked to the production relationships; for example, the owners' interests differ from those of the wage-earners. Because of class interests, class ideologies are created; that is, various views of the world are produced by the production relationships.

Societal organization and policy refer to all social relations, whereas "politics" refers to organizations and behavior related to the formal acquisition and exercise of power in a given social system. The social classes, for example, are part of the societal organization, but the electoral system is more particularly concerned with politics. Societal organization is deeply influenced by economic affairs. The economic organization of the Roman Empire, for example, produced relationships between masters and slaves. These can be compared to the relationships between owners and workers created in nineteenth-century Europe by the free-enterprise industrial system.

The prevailing economic organization, therefore, largely determines the types of relationships that exist between citizens. Among these relationships we must note those of domination. Some of these arise directly from the economic organization. This is obvious in the case of slaves and masters, but it is the same in a system of production based on the private ownership of the means of production, which, in the final analysis, gives the owners power over the non-owners. Here also a master-slave type of relationship arises almost immediately from an economic relationship.

## Ideological legitimization

Although social and political conditions develop with some autonomy, they are, as we have seen, partly determined by economic affairs. Social relationships, however, and especially relationships of domination, could not be maintained for long if they were not legitimized in some way. Capitalist society, for example, could not survive without an ideology that defends private ownership of the means of production. Without such an ideology, those who do not possess anything would react. The ideology of the private ownership of the means of production serves to legitimize the social system. In other words, beyond the political and economic system, there is an ideological system. Although it is to a certain extent autonomous from the other systems, its main function is to represent and justify the way in which society is organized. Generally it conceals some of the dominant relationships inherent in that social organization.

Although it is rather obvious, this last function of ideologies deserves deeper study. For this purpose, I shall offer a
structural comparison between prostitution and an employment contract. We shall see how the structures of these two
social relationships are very similar, but how, thanks to the
ideology of the private ownership of the means of production, they have very different values in society. In both cases,
a person exchanges something that is an intimate part of
himself or herself to somebody else for money. In the first
case, the use of one's body is sold to another, leaving to the
other person the decision of how to enter into a relationship
with that body. In the second case, workers relinquish control over their creativity and allow the boss to decide what
they should do. After all, as people say, the worker is paid for
that. In both situations, some persons give up something that
may be considered very close to the center of their person-
alities (their bodies or their creativity) by hiring it out to
another. The greatest difference between these two relationships is that, in our culture, the ideology of the private ownership of the means of production legitimizes the one, while
nothing legitimizes the other. Thus an ideology of production, in this case the ideology of private property, hides the
similarity between two very similar situations.

To illustrate the link between ideology, ethical standards, and types of production, let us consider what has
been called the puritan work ethic. At the end of the Middle
Ages, the way in which work was perceived changed in the
West. Although it had been valued to a certain extent for
some time, at this period it came to be held even more highly.
In protestant societies first of all—probably because they
were the most "modern"—work was proclaimed as one of
the most important values, which God would reward. Little
by little, work came to be considered not only a means of living, but an aim in itself. Thus a work ethic was born; its
effects are still to be seen today, for instance in the way in

which the unemployed are made to feel guilty. The fact of not working has in itself become a kind of a sin.

The advent of the work ethic can be linked to a deep transformation in society around that time: the division of labor. At the end of the Middle Ages, a merchant society was born in which roles diversified and in which, little by little, craftsmen's products came to be distributed and sold by others. In the industrial society, this division of labor intensified, and production was transformed. It was no longer directly related to the production of goods necessary to the group itself, as it had been on the self-sufficient farms. The work of one group now became necessary to others, and it therefore became part of a broader social network. Whereas in the Medieval farm people could immediately see why they had to work, under the division of labor the reasons for working only became apparent through social relationships. Work was no longer only useful to oneself and one's closest relations, but had become necessary to the life of society. To support this social organization, therefore, people had to be stimulated to work, because the usefulness of their labor was no longer directly apparent. This is probably how, through countless unconscious processes, the ideology that overvalues work was born. Compensation had to be provided at the ideological level for the loss of motivation resulting from the division of labor. In this way, ethics came to the aid of a commercial society in which a person's usefulness was not as apparent as it had been in the agrarian society. This ethic was necessary to support the socioeconomic order. And, in accordance with a well-known process, the less aware people were of the direct usefulness of their labor, the more ideology had to stress the sacredness of labor. What was at stake was not so much the work itself as the social bond underlying it. The puritan work ethic, according to this analysis, is therefore a result—at the ideological level—of the economic division of labor. Similar considerations could also be made concerning other ethical standards. We shall meet them in a later chapter, for example, in connection with the morality of emotional relationships.

Ideologies play an important role in maintaining a society's integrity and cohesion. Without them, the oppressed, and sometimes even the oppressor, would revolt, and in the end the political system and the type of production itself would be changed. That is why every society produces ethical codes that become tools for ideological domination. They give the oppressed an image of themselves that encourages them to stay "in their place," that is, oppressed. And in fact (we already analyzed this) it is often the most heavily dominated who are the greatest defenders of the ideologies that keep them dominated. We have seen above how ideological domination works: it deprives the oppressed of any possibility of imagining their lives other than they are, and a fortiori of thinking for themselves.

The oppressed are not the only ones who do not dare to think for themselves. Many people only think in reaction to something and depend heavily on the dominant ideologies. This can sometimes be a way of protecting social status or privileges. That is how what Nietzsche called the morals of slaves are formed. Those who dare not live for themselves— the slaves—manage, in spite of everything, to defend ethical systems; they justify their dependence and even value it, while expressing their resentment of free people. This slave morality is characterized by the fact that those who live it cannot imagine themselves making free decisions. On the contrary, they cannot do anything except by legitimizing their actions through a certain number of moral codes, religions, or even through science. They have such an image of themselves that any attempt to get out of their strait jackets seems extremely dangerous and is generally condemned. Furthermore, these "slaves" identify themselves so well with these systems that they punish those who refuse to accept the accepted codes. As an example, we have only to consider how aggressive some women are toward those who do not accept the standards of "womanhood." The "slave morality" thus introduces a unidimensional universe in which the dominant ideologies provide an answer for everything.

Marcuse described the technocratic, technological, and scientific society as unidimensional. Technocracy introduces a social balance by putting everything in its place according to a so-called "scientific" order. Then, insofar as one forgets how normative ideas are produced, everyone believes that everything is appropriately ordered in an eternal and universal world. If people, for example, wonder how to act, they will try to find the answer in psychology as a science; in the same way economy, as a science, will be normative in another area of life. In our technocratic society, human relations are filtered in the name of science by a moralizing ideological system that mediates any encounter between people. Positive encounters, as well as conflicts, are thus diluted by the sciences, by ethical codes, and by common knowledge. According to Marcuse, our society is characterized, then, by this reign of scientific rationalism to which everyone eventually has to submit.

It should be pointed out that, because of the relative independence of the ideological systems with respect to the economic and political dimensions of society, an ideology can continue to exist when what produced it has disappeared. Sometimes one comes across moral values that seem "strange," because there does not seem to be any link between them and the way that society functions today. They are traces of the past.

### Marx: dialectics or reduction?

Contrary to certain popularizations, Marx does not reduce ideological and political matters to economics by some mechanical kind of production; rather, he recognizes the reciprocal and dialectic relations between the different levels. Thus, the economic system may produce the political system, but the political system in turn influences the economic system. Political and social changes may eventually bring about changes in the type of production. For example, a powerful military class can be the result of a search for economic stability, but this military class can modify the economic organization. Similarly, the ideological system may profoundly influence the sociopolitical or economic systems.

What Marx does state is that, in the final analysis, the economic system does determine the whole. By "in the final analysis," I simply mean this: a society could not exist if it could not produce what is necessary for its survival. If this means that the economic aspect is fundamental, other levels may, according to the type of society being considered, carry more or less weight. That is why Althusser speaks of *dominant* and *determining* aspects; in his opinion, while the economic aspect is, in the final analysis, determinant, the ideological or political aspects may be dominant. Thus, in our industrial society, the dominant level is economic. In the feudal system, the political aspect was the most important for the structuring of society. In Palestine in the days of Jesus Christ, the ideological system, through its religious aspects (the temple, the law, and the prophets) predominated.

Marx's essential merit might be his having recognized a precise and detectable, if not always explicable, link between the ideological, political, and economic levels. Although most people think that ideas, standards, and moral codes are purely and simply the products of thinkers, Marx showed that the consistency of ideologies could only be explained by a dialectic link to the political and economic levels.

### For a non-idealistic theory of the production of notions

Notions do not come from nowhere; they are related to the social groups that produce them. The question is, how do they emerge and what is their role? What can such concepts as "friendship," "responsibility," or any of the others currently used in ethics mean?

We shall start from the existence, in any culture, of a set of stories that are told to people from their childhood. Let us just think, for example, of "Donald Duck," "The Velveteen Rabbit"—or the Bible. These stories gradually shape the minds of those who hear them and structure the universe in which they live. Through them, people continuously tell their own stories. What we know of people's lives is never what has "really" happened (what does this word "really" mean, anyway?), but *stories* of their lives. The same event can be recounted in many ways, and indeed it is narrated through cultural representations, that is, other stories that are present in the culture. For example, we read about the events of the Ides of March 44 B.C. as a story of assassination; but what if we were told about the death of Caesar as a story of an execution? In more general terms, it can be said that every time we interpret events, we do so by attaching them to other stories, which give them meaning.

In order to understand better the way in which stories work to produce ideas and concepts, let us look at the concept of love. We start from the existence of a certain class of stories: love stories. There is quite a collection of them, ranging from the story of a prostitute trying to find meaning in her life to the biography of a mystic. The concept of love is linked to this set of stories present in our culture. The way in which these stories are related to each other depends on our culture. In some societies one story will be considered part of a set of love stories, whereas in another it will belong to a different set of stories. Indeed, differences of opinion may arise; some people will call a story a "love story" and others will not. But what is important in the long run is that there are sets of stories and that human beings use them. They use their collection of stories to tell their own story. They say, for instance, "My story is also a love story," and, in fact, as they tell it they consciously or unconsciously link it to other love stories they have read or heard.

To what extent could I talk about my love life if there were not previous love stories to which I can refer? This can be seen when adolescents start to live their first love. They may experience certain events without calling them a love story. Boys say they would like to meet a particular girl and find her intelligent and pretty; quite "by chance," they are often together. They share a certain relationship but do not perceive it as belonging to the category of love. Then there may come a time when they say, "But in fact, all this means I am in love." At the moment when adolescents say "I am in love," what happens is not a change in what they are experiencing, but rather a change in their way of "reading" what they are experiencing, which is now linked to other love stories. On the one hand, they realize that they are in love, that is, they read their experience differently. And on the other hand, thanks to the experience they are living through, they begin to understand the love stories that they had heard previously. Indeed, before people can talk about their life as a love story, love stories appear foreign to them, are often difficult to understand, and are sometimes even meaningless. However, when people start using these stories to understand their own story, and when these stories make their own story more intelligible, then they understand them. There is, therefore, a kind of dialectic bond between peoples' experience and the stories present in their culture. Before linking their own experience to stories that help them to understand it, adolescents are incapable of talking about their experience. It is impossible for them to talk about themselves without referring to a story already present in their culture. Similarly, before they live the experience that they will recognize in love stories, love stories seem meaningless to them. So one's experience, read in stories, finds meaning at the same time that these stories find content. A dialectic link is established between a concrete experience and the stories present in a culture.

It is therefore thanks to previously existing stories in our culture that we become able to read our own story and experience. Without these stories, experience seems meaningless, that is, it cannot be the subject of a story. This is how such general concepts as love are born; the concept refers to the collection of stories that gives it its meaning. One can talk about love as soon as one links an experience with that collection of stories. From this point of view, a concept appears to be that which links together culturally, and therefore always slightly artificially, a series of stories told in a given culture. Seen in this light, there is obviously no concept of love in itself. All we are aware of is a series of love stories that may allow other people to tell their own story and add it to the culture's collection, which in the end is the basis for the concept. There is a dialectic link between people's behavior and the stories and theories that make it intelligible. Indeed, stories on their own appear empty, if they have no link with the practices of the people who live them. Furthermore, an act that cannot be recounted is an experience that, literally, has no meaning; it is a blind act that cannot be "socialized" among fellow human beings. What produces meaning, therefore, is the stories and, therefore, the people who recount their lives. But these stories are not invented out of nothing; on the contrary, people use literary forms, older stories, and myths carried by the culture.

Understood in this way, notions no longer appear as normative, but rather as social facts that are present in the culture. Ideas are there as stories; we depend on them because we cannot understand our own story without referring to them. But nothing forces us to limit ourselves to a particular type of story to describe our own existence. We can select from all the stories available to tell our own, which thus becomes original. Many stories that, from certain points of view, may have little in common with each other, can thus be considered as love stories. One can take extreme cases, such as two adolescents who discover love in a car contrasted with married couples who have spent their whole lives together. Each has a very different story to tell; and yet our culture puts them together in the same category. Yet some people will not want to see their story as one that can be compared to a love story lived out in a car, while others will accept such a comparison. These stories are therefore not normative; rather, they offer possible ways of interpreting people's lives. When a large number of stories is available to us, we can (at least to a certain extent) choose what kind we want to take as a model for our lives. In all cases, the type of story our life will make will be somewhat different from the type we chose as a model. However, particular stories can play an important role for particular people, because of the possibilities they open for understanding and building their existence.

What I have stated about the concept of love is equally true for other concepts, for example, that of responsibility. This concept includes stories of people who, in our culture, are considered to have lived responsible lives. It is this collection of stories that, once again, determines the content of the concept of responsibility. Certain people may say to themselves, "The way in which I understand my story resembles closely that of people who have acted 'in a responsible way' within our culture." From that moment on, they begin to "read" their own experience in such a way as to be able to recount it with that meaning.

Conversely, it is interesting to see how difficult it is for people to live through situations for which there are no stories that enable them to verbalize what they wish to live out. These stories, which the sociologists sometimes call "cultural models," are wanting. This is true, for example, in our culture for the new ways of living family life or engagements. The model of the family is evolving, but when people speak of the family, they refer to a set of stories that no longer reflects the experience that many people have had or would like to have. They therefore find it difficult to tell their story: they don't have any ready-made stories, but have to make up their own from bits and pieces. They have to construct and invent their lives, with little help from the culture. This often requires much energy on their part, because many of them doubt the legitimacy of their story. They hesitate to listen to the type of stories they want to tell because, in a given culture, some stories are accepted as legitimate and normal while others are rejected.

### Variety of readings

According to what has been stated above, one can try to "reach" people's practices in several ways. In fact, we never know what has "really happened." The same events, "read" by different observers, can lead to entirely different stories; it is impossible to speak about the "real" event. What some perceive as an extremely courageous sacrifice, others consider insanity or madness. Insofar as one believes that there are no such things as eternal ideas, there are no criteria, outside history, for preferring one reading over another. The activities of human beings thus appear as a reference for many stories with several different interpretations.

The stories will be all the more different because they are the result of reading through different frames of reference or paradigms. By "frames of reference," I mean ways in which the telling of one story is, through the selection of events, linked to other stories. For example, one can speak of a frame of reference for a psychological interpretation, through which an event will be interpreted according to the criteria of individual psychology, and individual elements will be stressed. When I wish to speak about suicide using a psychological frame of reference, I shall show the dynamics of an individual suicide. The same event could also be interpreted according to a sociological frame of reference, which will help me to perceive better the sociological forces that lead to a certain percentage of suicides in a region.

According to the types of accounts in which we include the story of certain events, the events will appear more or less different. If, for example, a relationship is considered as being of the professional type, it will have one interpretation. But if that same relationship is considered as being one of love, it will have another interpretation. There are several possible frames of reference for the same event; each of them will give a different account of the events, and, in the end, indicate a different meaning. By "meaning," we refer here to the way in which stories can be integrated into others and thus linked to each other. It should be remembered that, from the point of view described here, giving meaning to an event implies that one's story can be understood through other stories, which are thus used as references for meaning.[2] The event, in its "pure state," is often referred to as the "sig-

2. Thus a "Christian meaning to existence" refers to a reading of existence with reference to stories of the life of Christ.

nified" (or "thing signified"). But it obviously does not exist as such and cannot be apprehended in this way. To understand an event and to be able to talk about it one has to say "something" about it, in other words, put it into a story. The event as linked to other stories, as something with a meaning, is then called "significant" (or "that which gives meaning").

If there are many different accounts, there are also many different meanings for events. These meanings often conflict with each other. The same events are not interpreted as if they intended to express the same reality. The way in which an account is handled in order to give a definite meaning to events is the object of ideological struggle; the "reading" of a story is never neutral, but always done with a purpose. There is, therefore, always a variety of readings, with a variety of meanings and perhaps conflicts about the way of reading.

The way certain events are interpreted also depends on one's position in relation to them. Thus, when one has to recount an event that is known as a strike—at least according to certain readings[3]—there will be totally different accounts depending on whether one adopts the boss's or the workers' point of view. And in the end the meaning attributed to it will be different. The reading in that case depends on the social position of a person or a group, and not only on the individual position. Consequently, the readings made of these events do not only depend on individual wishes but also on social interests, that is to say, on one's place in the social structure. In a university classroom, for example, the wishes of students can be very different and can induce different readings of the situation. But the very structure of a classroom divides those present into at least two categories, faculty and students. Because of this social situation, the interests of the instructor and the students diverge, at least to a

3. In other readings, it could be spoken of as, for example, a lack of realism.

certain extent. We are no longer confronted with individual wishes alone, but also with class interests,[4] that is, interests determined by the production relationships and organization of the university. Because of this, teachers and students tend to make different readings of realities; these are class-based readings. An example of this is when the same behavior is described as "laziness" by the teacher and "lack of interest in a boring course" by the student. Different readings, therefore, are not only produced by divergent wishes, but also by the positions in society that determine the wishes.

### The ideological production of stories

In the preceding section, we saw how stories make it possible to "read" events. We showed how this reading is one of several possible ones, that is to say, there are several ways of telling one's lived experience. In order to understand society, it is important that all its subgroups discover which stories are the most used, which are the most widely accepted and acceptable for describing what happens. These most widespread stories reflect the ideology that society, and especially its dominant groups, tends to produce. They are a witness to the image that society has of itself. This becomes clear when a country pays historians to write its history, that is, to interpret events in order to legitimize the present political situation. This version of history is always related to the interests of the dominant groups of society. One only has to see how, every time a conquest or a revolution takes place, history books are automatically rewritten in order to provide a new reading of what has happened.

Society also produces stories that enable people to describe their own lives. Generally speaking, the production of these stories is what makes ethics. Indeed, speaking about

4. In orthodox Marxism, we cannot speak of classes when talking about the divergent interests between lecturers and students.

ethics, about morals, means presenting stories that can be used by others to construct and tell their own stories. Seen in this light, ethical discourse does not necessarily present obligations. Ethics appear, not as standards, but as possibilities or even as an appeal to those who could make their story into one similar to the story being told. For example, giving an ethical discourse on sexuality means saying how sexuality can be lived and presenting stories that may become typical or ideal for those who, in their turn, will later want to tell the story of their own sexual life.[5] This kind of ethical discourse is not necessarily normative. It does, however, always emerge from and reflect the views of a given society and a particular standpoint in that society. Thus stories about manhood and womanhood will always bear traces of their origins. In our Western society, a story coming from a group that supports men's role in society will be quite different from one coming from a group of feminists. Stories concerning masculinity and femininity are therefore not neutral, because they are never seen from a detached point of view, but rather are situated in the midst of social conflicts concerning woman's place in a society dominated by man.

Seen in this light, stories may be taken as calls emerging from particular standpoints. Any story can be situated in this way, even comic strips. The adventures of Donald Duck, for example, present a kind of middle-class ideal. One only has to read them to see how biased the contents are. *Jonathan Livingston Seagull* carries a similar heavy ideological content. It could only be written in a society where achievement is given a high value. Stories concerning the ethics of commerce also betray their origins; for example, they draw very important distinctions between different ways of taking money out of other people's pockets. The label "theft," with

5. We should point out that the very concept of sexuality can only be defined with reference to a certain number of stories: it is also a culture-based concept.

very pejorative overtones, is attached to the action of taking a ten-dollar bill out of one's neighbor's pocket, whereas taking a million dollars out of many people's pockets is considered "good business"! We can see through this that ethical discourse offers ways of living that are linked to particular social positions and interests, rather than universal ideals. Ethical discourse is, therefore, a call, but a call that can only be understood if it is also related to the interests it represents. Statements that seem purely "ethical" and free of relation to social interests are no exception. Thus, sociologists have shown that the ethics of marriage are associated with the sociopolitical and economic organization of Western patriarchal society.

From the point of view presented here, society has a certain structure in which social actors call others to action. Ethical discourse is not so much a disinterested theory presenting eternal values as a committed ideological production that affects society. This vision of ethics is different from the traditional view, according to which morals say "what must be done," implying obligations. From the sociologist's point of view, obligatory morals are often little more than thinly disguised sociopolitical and ideological domination. Indeed, inasmuch as ethicists dictate what must be done, they are working in behalf of the particular social order that they are thus promoting. This raises some questions regarding situations where legislators dictate what should be done. What are the relationships between laws and ethics?

# 4

# LAW—JUSTICE AND SOCIETY

## The foundations of law

"Justice has been done." That is what we often hear said when the defendant has been sentenced and taken off to prison. What is the basis of this "justice" and this "law," according to which some people can be found guilty and put in prison? Are the guilty punished because they have done something wrong? Are they a danger to society? Or have certain other people decided, out of their own interests, to put them away?

There are several conceptions of law and of justice. Without claiming to be exhaustive, I will divide them into three conceptual categories: the *natural*; the *positivist* and *technocratic*; and the *positive* and *political*. The last, in my opinion, is the most satisfactory.

## Human nature and criteria of good and evil

The notion of natural justice is based on the concept of natural law, according to which human society is built in accordance with an *aim*, predetermined either by "human nature" or by what is useful. This aim (which is often only apprehended implicitly) is related to a certain understanding of good and evil: actions that accord with human nature or utility are good, and all others are bad. In the perspective of natural justice, the legal system should be linked as closely as possible to the accepted definition of good and evil. A good legal system punishes bad actions and encourages good ones.

Lawmakers who accept the natural law premise try to draw up the best possible laws. They therefore implicitly presuppose a set of criteria that they believe makes it possible to decide in a universal, nonpartisan way what is good and what is bad. Of course, they recognize the difficulties in formulating an ideal law, but this utopian background always underlies and regulates their lawmaking activities. Several tendencies are included under this general classification of natural justice, including utilitarianism, which considers it possible to determine objectively and in an unbiased way the best solution to a problem. All these doctrines have to be precisely defined, but their common feature is the one we mentioned: a normative concept of a common good.

In this perspective, the basis of good and evil is perceived differently according to the philosophical beliefs of the lawmakers. For some it depends on God's plan for creation; for others it is derived from human nature, utility, reason, or the common good; for all who use this approach it depends, in the final analysis, on an authority that is situated beyond any partisan or self-interested position. It is precisely this claim to universality that modern movements of critical thought dispute, raising a new question concerning the law: whose—which group's—welfare does it promote?

In order to understand criticisms of the natural justice concept, it might be useful to examine the idea of "common good." This notion is often invoked by people who wish to create legislation; laws are supposed to serve the common good. The concept then seems to operate as if a common good exists, fixed once and for all, universally. In extreme cases, this idealistic concept may claim to form the basis of a natural law, a law that legislation should promote.

The theory of ideologies, however, casts doubts on this concept. It is indeed difficult to see how such a universal concept could work, since any specific solution implies a definition of the common good in terms of the criteria and interests of a particular group. For example, when it is baldly stated that "scientific and technical progress promote the common good," this global view considers as negligible the particular welfare of those who will become unemployed as a result of this technical progress.[1] Obviously the final result of this "common good" is not the good of all; it is common only in the context of a particular hierarchy of values. Let us take another example: the economic measure that will save a country from inflation will cause bankruptcy for a number of people. For them, what does "common good" mean? It is obviously not their good. These examples show that as soon as one tries to define the common good in any precise way, it never includes *the good of everyone*, and that choices are made among the diverse interests of certain people and groups. For all practical purposes, then, any concrete manifestation of the "common good" always refers in the end to the more limited concept of "the good of the society as defined by certain groups." Of course this does not prevent the

1. Other examples can be cited: ethnic minorities, racial minorities, homosexuals, ecologists, and so on.

distinction from being made between the individual good and what might be called "the good of society." The latter notion could be defined as that good for which the good of some individuals is sacrificed in the name of the good and the interests of other individuals. What is important to understand is that this "good of society" is always defined by groups or individuals. It is never a given fact; it is a program of action that certain people offer and support.

This brief discussion shows that it is impossible to base law on the "nonpartisan" concept of the common good, since everything presented under that name has been thought out and elaborated according to certain particular social perspectives. The law implies choices and these choices are political in nature. Yet some groups claim that it is possible to determine the common good in a *universal* way, based either on rationality or on religion. But rationality applied in these cases always flows from a set of presuppositions that *depends on the social standpoint of those who apply it*.[2] And the very number of bodies of law based on religion shows clearly how particularized they are in nature. Consequently, the idea of common good can be considered as an ideological concept inasmuch as it conceals the very relative and particularized nature of the origins of social programs presented as "common" ones. Any program for society is structured according to the interests of some groups, and it is hard to see how these particular plans can claim the right to be imposed on everyone in the name of "common good," at least if by common good we mean the good of all.

However, it is not by chance that, in the name of common good, the law is often presented as the vehicle of moral requirements expressed as good and evil. Indeed, such a legitimation of the law and of the program for society that is

2. For a more systematic account of the way in which scientific presuppositions always carry ideological biases, see my book *La Science Partisane* (Gembloux: Duculot, 1974).

linked to it enables those who promulgate it to preserve their own social order. In fact, as we shall see, the law is a social compromise imposed by a majority or, more accurately, by a dominant group. The power that imposes it is disguised. Indeed, the interests at stake are concealed in proportion to the extent to which the law is experienced as a *moral* requirement, or as a vehicle for the common good. As Rousseau pointed out, the strongest man is never strong enough to be always the master unless he changes his strength into a right, and obedience into a duty.

### The positivist and technocratic conception

Faced with the inadequacy of the universal concepts of common good and natural law, some lawyers consider law according to a positivist, technocratic perspective. In their view, an ethical or political meaning should not be sought for any legal rule. Rather, the rule exists, and that is all the lawyer needs to know. All that he need do is make it work consistently, without asking further questions. This point of view has one real advantage over the natural law concept: because law is presented as a matter of fact, it is not moralizing, and consequently it adds no ideological domination to the sovereignty of the rule of law. In a natural law concept of justice, when someone is sent to prison it is claimed that he is evil, because he has broken the rules that express good and evil. In a positivist conception, he is sent to prison simply because he has not obeyed the law, and no more questions are asked. The law is a technique and is accepted as such. It is considered better not to think about its origins. Apparently we could conclude that a positivist legal system has one advantage over law based on natural justice: while both represent the common good of a particular group, at least one of them does not claim to have universal value.

And yet, although the positivist conception hides less of reality than the natural law conception, it leaves unanswered a number of questions. Who establishes the rules for the legal system, and why? How does one take up one's position in relation to these rules? How can one deal with ideological disagreements felt in relation to the concept of the common good, which underlies these rules? In short, the positivist conception looks very weak when it comes to giving "legitimacy" to the law. Inasmuch as it does not concern itself with the foundations of the law, it is completely incapable of answering social questions related to its legitimacy. What difference is there between rules promulgated by a so-called "legitimate" government and by a Mafia boss? What difference is there between a common-law crime and a political crime? A positivist conception of law, which presupposes a clear boundary between political and judicial affairs, ignores these thorny problems. Yet precisely this kind of question is the concern of another conception of law: the positive and political theory, as expounded by many thinkers, including Max Weber.[3]

### Order established by the dominant group

Characteristic of Weber's thought about legal systems and the law is a change of sociological perspective. His approach attaches greater importance to how the law really works than to how it is said to work. Thus, Weber's first statement is that underlying the law is a force that alone gives it the capacity to govern people. At first sight this force, which is inherent in the law, is not very different from brute force. And yet, thanks to long-standing habit and the dominant ide-

---

3. When I refer to the Weberian conception of the law, I do not mean to discuss that author's doctrines. I am simply using the term to describe a conception that can, to a certain degree, be derived from his work.

ology, most citizens are virtually unaware of the fact that behind the law there lies the force required for its application.

This change of perspective by which one can begin to perceive the force behind the law can be illustrated by a passage from *The Godfather*.[4] Mike, the son of the head of a Mafia family, is engaged to Kay, an Anglo-Saxon. Somewhat disturbed by the activities of her fiancé's family, she asks Mike, "But what, in fact, does your father do?" Mike replies, "My father is a bit like a governor, a senator—someone who looks after people's welfare." Kay, surprised, exclaims, "But senators and governors don't have people killed!" Then Mike, with a smile that is both ironic and condescending, says, "Kay, you are very naive!"

In fact, Weber's conception of law is well illustrated by the whole of Puzo's novel. Situating the Mafia within the context of American society, Puzo describes how American law protected its own kind while keeping the Italian immigrants on the fringes. The common good of the Americans was not for the common good of the Italian immigrants. The novel shows how, confronted with this situation, a young immigrant decides to set up his own order to defend the good of the Italians. Thus the Mafia is born, with its own system of laws. For anybody as intelligent as Mike, the position is clear: on the one hand the senators and governors defend their rights and their order with legal force, and on the other hand the Mafia defends the rights and the order of the Italians with illegal force. In this way, we all live within several systems of law, because every subgroup we belong to tends to claim its own rights, and some of them are contradictory.

That, broadly speaking, is the Weberian conception of the law: the law is the rule that the dominant group of a society, which has the power to have it enforced, decrees. According to this point of view, the law derives its power from

4. Mario Puzo, *The Godfather* (New York: Putnam, 1969); released as a film by Paramount Pictures in 1972.

the dominant group's ability to impose and apply its "social compromise." And, in the end, the reason why people are sent to prison is not that they have done something wrong (one might wonder, moreover, who would define what "wrong" is), but that they are considered a threat to the order the dominant group has established.

At first sight, this might seem a very bold conception; our minds are so used to referring to values and higher authorities, or even to religion, for our laws. And yet anyone who examines in detail how the law functions will soon realize that Weber's description is not the caricature it first appears to be. As we mentioned earlier, for example, taking money from one's neighbor—is that a sufficient motive for imprisonment? It seems obviously so, but there are distinctions. Taking a few hundred dollars is called stealing. However, if you get away with hundreds of thousands—something that can be done in many different ways—that is called "good business." And when we look more closely, we realize that what is punished is not the appropriation of one's neighbor's wealth, but a certain *way* of appropriating it, a way that is not acceptable to the established order. We can see that the force of the law comes to the aid of the social compromise that dominant groups or a majority have managed to impose. Calling upon a moral power for the law seems to be a mystification that protects the dominant order. Without that mystification, in many cases a society's ruling classes would be unable to maintain their power over a majority whose interests are not protected in the established order.

One may, however, wonder whether this way of thinking can be extended to the law in all its functions. In other words, if the Weberian view explains the way legislation works for private property, should we not accept that it does not explain laws to punish really "evil" offences, such as attacks on old persons or on children? Indeed, in such cases doesn't the law punish a real "evil," something universally reprehensible? The Weberian conception actually claims to explain obvious differences, such as the difference between a simple theft and a wicked crime, without having recourse to a universal concept of evil. That difference stems from the fact that, in our society, nearly everybody accepts a law that punishes certain crimes considered as "wicked," while in cases that involve robbing the rich (for example), only those who have internalized the ideology concerning private property accept the law as just. What makes the difference is not the wicked character of some crimes, but the existence of unanimous disapproval of them.

Anthropologists confirm this analysis. They point out, for example, that no society, and certainly not our own, would punish the pure and simple fact of "killing," but only certain *ways* of killing that are not accepted insofar as they question the order established by the dominant group in society. The fact that senators killed by having bombs dropped on North Vietnam in no way threatened American society and does not seem to have been against the law. In some societies, the distinction is much clearer: only near relatives are protected from murder by the law; the law protects the neighbor, not the stranger. We can thus see how even the proscription of murder can depend on the structure of social relationships.

### Justice and politics

The Weberian conception is particularly helpful when it comes to understanding the difficult distinction between common-law crimes and political crimes. One can claim that all crimes are political if by that one means that they are violations of the dominant order. But in a deeper analysis the distinction works in a very simple way, without our falling back upon universal concepts of the common good. Political crimes are crimes that are repressed as part of the internal tensions and conflicts over power in society. Common-law crimes, on the other hand, are violations of the order established by the dominant ideology, which defines right and wrong in the society. This is where we can define a concept of the common good that does not claim to be universal. Indeed, insofar as a group fears the unknown and the unexpected, it will prefer order to disorder and will be ready to sacrifice some interests to preserve the order that it will call the "common good." That is why it is quite consistent to accept or to impose an order, even if it is only a relative one. By unmasking the claim to a universal basis for law, the Weberian conception by no means argues for anarchy. It simply shows the ambiguity and the inherent risks in any expansion of power underlying new legislation.

### Justice as a reflection of the balance of power

In societies in which the delineation between the judicial and the political branches is less clearly drawn than our own, the Weberian model is much more obvious. Louis XIV said: "I am the state." When monarchs or oligarchs impose their will, it has the force of law. What is punishable, then, is anything that displeases the prince. To send somebody to the Bastille, the kings of France had no need of any other motive than their displeasure. Any ideology of the divine right of kings could make all that legitimate. But in less centralized states, in which power belongs to certain classes of citizens, mediation becomes necessary. Another type of ideological authority is then resorted to, in order to legitimize the power of the dominant group, but its mechanics are basically the same: the law punishes those who threaten the established order. It can be noticed that the law never takes up the defense of those who do not themselves possess a certain power to defend themselves. For example, it is only when workers have acquired real power for themselves by modifying the power relationships that the law recognizes their rights. Similarly, it is only because some people really take the interests of the poor to heart that they are beginning to acquire rights too. Or again, ethnic minorities in general do not have any rights until they have sufficient support from within the power structure.

There is in society a clear distinction between those who have rights and those who do not, or, in other words, between those who identify with the dominant groups and those who do not. This split becomes obvious when I ask myself: "Would it be normal if I, for some reason or other, were to find myself in jail one day?" Part of the population would immediately reply, "I will never be, unless a catastrophe happens." In another section of the population, however, people can quite easily imagine themselves being locked up. This distinction is particularly illustrative in a racist country in which the mere fact of being black considerably increases one's likelihood of one day going to prison. In this case the dominant group indeed shows its true colors!

Although one cannot always draw such clear lines, it is obvious that, in general, the way legislation and justice work is a faithful reflection of the balance of power in the society being examined.

According to this very positive and political conception, it seems that, in the final analysis, law expresses the will of the dominant groups in society. Ideologies, however, disguise that fact and the real balance of power. But the latter becomes obvious in times of crisis. Of course, even then attempts are always made to conceal what is going on by calling on many legitimating reasons; but there are times when it becomes clear that the law's only reason for being is the force that upholds it. This is the case with coups d'état.

The Weberian conception of law thus demystifies justice. However, one important detail must be made clear: although it demonstrates clearly the link between law and force, the Weberian understanding is far removed from anarchistic criticism that calls the law useless and denounces any use of force to preserve the established order. For such anarchists, any power or force is bad, or, paradoxically, is attributed to some kind of moralizing authority. The Weberian conception simply describes the place of force in conflicts of interest. In this perspective, the order of the Mafia or of American society should be classed, not among conflicts of universal values, but among conflicts of interests and blueprints for society. In any plan for a society, the defense of a certain order is always involved. There will therefore always be an imposed *law*; and even under regimes that claim to be permissive, there is always a certain repression (even if only "It is forbidden to forbid"). The difference is not to be found in the existence of an imposed law, but in the ideology that legitimizes it: either as a welfare that is claimed to be universal, or as a welfare that is defined by a particular vision.

## The need for law

Among societies that have developed a legal system, even those that largely dispense with brute force cannot do everything they please. Acquired rights, embodied in the law, have an important mobilizing effect. (President Nixon learned this during the Watergate affair.) A legal code, accepted as legitimate (and in the final analysis, simply *accepted*), is thus a protection against arbitrary subjective will, and thereby represents a real defense of society. It basically sets up a code for social interplay. Since it is difficult to play when there are no rules or when the rules are always changing, the boundary between what is legal and what is not is important. Outside what is legal (according to whatever law), another person's actions are no longer predictable. Life becomes insecure for everybody, it is war. Furthermore, as we shall see later, mediation by the rule of law protects human relations from anarchy and from paternalism, thus introducing an idea of justice that is different from love.

Within a given legal framework, the dominant groups and the masters can no longer do exactly as they please. The legal structure mobilizes enough energy to force them to give up brute force. As a result, although the law may in a given (synchronic) analysis appear to the sociologist as an expression of the balance of power, the politician and the person engaged in concrete action will see law as the result—no doubt temporary, but having a certain stability—of their struggles. This is obvious in the area of labor, where workers speak frequently about winning their rights.

In a broader sense, any law is a codified, precise compromise between different interests. It will have the full functions of a law if it attracts enough power to enforce its application. However, even without such physical force, any recognized codification produces an ideological force. That is why the United Nations Human Rights Charter, however imperfect and imprecise it may be, still makes a difference. It makes possible a more precise point of reference than the simple vague idea of respect for human beings. This is a sufficiently important example to warrant further examination.

### The ambiguity of human rights

The concept of human rights is both very ambiguous and very important. It is very ambiguous because it can refer to vastly different kinds of social behavior and projects. Speaking of these rights means recognizing that there is a minimum requirement for human life that should be granted to everyone. Since this minimum requirement is often expressed in biological terms (food, clothing, shelter, and so on), we often speak of natural needs and then of natural rights. This is why human rights are often discussed from a natural justice point of view. The very term "human rights" (in French, the "rights of man") is significant. It presupposes a normative conception of the human being and of humanity, without its being realized that this typified human is usually quite simply made in the image of and in favor of the dominant group in society. That is why only too often human rights are just one more means by which the privileged defend their privileges. This is no doubt the case when people talk about the right to choose their own doctor, the rights of the head of the family, the right to private property, the right to carry a gun, and so on. This was clearly illustrated by a historian of the Indian wars in the United States who spoke of "an incredible era of violence, greed, audacity, sentimentality, undirected exuberance, and almost reverential attitude toward the ideal of personal freedom for those who already had it."[5] That is what almost always arises when people deal with a vague, ideological concept, defined in a universal way, such as the concepts of human rights or freedom.

It is quite different when one talks about people's rights in a given social context: that is, as clearly defined, recognized rights in a society organized so as to defend them. These rights, once established (that is, when the force required to have them respected can be mobilized), fix real limits to the dominating power of the strong. That is why they are never given once and for all, but are the result of ongoing battles and struggles. To check their existence, therefore, one should not concentrate on the rights and privileges of the powerful, but on those of the humble, the oppressed, the foreigners. The extension of rights to the people is a long, historic struggle through which our most liberating societies have tried to defend the minimum needs of the oppressed.[6] The rights granted to each individual are meaning-

5. Dee Brown, *Bury My Heart at Wounded Knee: An Indian History of the American West* (New York: Holt, Rinehart and Winston, 1970), p. xv.

6. This movement obviously owes much to Christianity, which, at least in

ful when they are used to defend the humble in a situation of distress, whereas talking about human rights in order to organize and protect the privileges of the powerful is simply hypocritical.

Moreover, these human rights are never absolute; they are always related to a given context. It is not meaningful to talk about the right to liberty, to free speech, to health, or even to life at any price. But a society can guarantee specific rights, such as the right to health care, to being able to say what one thinks, to not being arrested without a warrant, to not losing one's job because of one's private opinions or one's race, and so forth. The struggle for rights, for their extension and their defense, is a perpetual one. The law establishes some points that the dominant groups of our society recognize, at least in theory if not always in practice, as limits to their arbitrary power. If it is true that the relationships between forces can always be perceived through rules of law, it must not be forgotten that the absence of rules leaves the field wide open for the total domination of complete arbitrariness. "When laws end, tyrannies begin."[7]

### Summary

"There is no justice!" That is true, if by "justice" one means a universal idea based on notions of "objectivity," of "good," and of "evil." Why are people sent to jail? It is usually because they are a threat to the established order that dominant groups impose on society. The laws reflect, not a universal common good, but rather those groups' projects and the concessions they have had to make to others to maintain a balance of power within their society. Law as an ideo-

---

theory and intention, has always paid special attention to the poorest members of society.

7. William Pitt, speech on the Wilkes case, January 9, 1770.

logical force is, however, very relevant. Once the law has been established, the mobilizing role ideologies play turns it into a point of reference that sets limits to brute force. There is nothing sacred about the law, and the "justice" it promotes has nothing universal about it. And yet it obviously plays an essential role among those factors that liberate humankind.

In the end of this chapter, a question should be raised: Where and how does ethics confront the legal system? My answer would be that there is no *general* ethics that can challenge the legal system from an absolute point of view. Laws can only be challenged by a *particular* ethical stand that stems from specific individuals or from specific groups. The temptation of any group or individual is to believe that its particular ethics always stem from some implicit choices or, more precisely, from the choice of standing in solidarity with some specific groups and their vested interests; an example is the choice of being in solidarity with the oppressed or with the powerful.

# 5

# OBLIGATORY MORALITY OR AMORALITY?

## An unreal dilemma

Those who speak of ethics without moral obligation are often told that they face a dilemma: either there are moral obligations that say exactly what has to be done, or there is total amorality. This is a false dilemma. It is indeed possible to make a moral judgment of an action, even when one has forsaken any universal distinction between what must be done and what must not be done, and even if the categories of good and evil have been rejected. For example, I could say, to paraphrase St. Paul, "Everything is allowed, but not necessarily good for me," and in this way move beyond the opposition between a compulsory ethics and amorality or moral indifference. There is another possibility beyond these two extremes in which, without necessarily being confronted by obligations, people nevertheless pull away from moral indifference because they receive a call that stems from a given source. This is what we mean by a "calling ethics."[1]

The fact that there is, in society, a variety of ethical calls challenges us to choose and eliminates the possibility of moral indifference. Options and choices that one can take are not arbitrary, because calls are addressed to those who have to act. And yet there is no question of a compulsory ethics.

Normative statements could be appropriately translated into calls that offer people a certain view of life. Such calls come from specific places and individuals in society. The meaning of actions, the ethical meaning, can be explained by examining how actions are related to these calls. We shall thus learn how a calling ethics works and see how it differs from a compulsory or a normative morality.

### Calling ethics

From the point of view of a calling ethics, the intersubjective world is considered as a field in which human beings make calls upon each other and communicate the meanings of their actions. Some say: "It is worth devoting one's life to earning money"; others say: "Only love gives any meaning to what I do"; still others say: "Reading the life of Buddha (or of Jesus Christ, or the works of Karl Marx or of St. Francis of Assisi or even, for some, of Hitler) gives me a framework for my existence." The way in which different people talk about their existence and interpret meanings also provides "frames of reference" for interpreting other lives. Thus, any existence is a kind of poem that can be read and interpreted. Everyone can also make their own existence into their own poem and, to express that story, fragments of other poems are used. To

1. This way of considering morals follows Henri Bergson (cf. "The Two Sources of Morality and Religion") or Marcel Legaut (cf. his concept of "calling religion").

the extent to which the story of someone else's life in particular is used, it can be said that somebody is living the poem or the mysteries of the other person's life. For example, a person who has been struck by the life of Buddha and his "compassion" will start interpreting his or her own life in those terms, and will perceive the life of Buddha as a call and will make a value out of that virtue. It should, moreover, be pointed out that compassion, in this case, will be understood in the context of Buddha's story, or at least in the framework of the poem his life represents. It is, however, important to point out that there is a difference between a life story and a call: the life story of Jesus is, for a Christian, a poem in which to situate one's life, whereas the Sermon on the Mount is more of a particular appeal from Jesus.

Seen in this light, the meaning of people's lives can no longer be considered as morally indifferent. Reading one's own life or the life of others always implies starting from a choice, the choice of the poem or the call that will give meaning to existence. Each individual's story asserts its own meaning through the variety of stories, poems, and calls carried in a given society, and each individual's story implies a stance vis-à-vis this multiplicity. It may find its place, for example, as a story of self-sacrifice or as a story of the accumulation of wealth. Different choices produce different societal histories and meanings. Human actions are therefore never morally neutral; they carry ethical meaning because they represent stances taken up before a variety of possibilities.

From the point of view of a calling ethic, therefore, no two actions are morally equivalent, even though no action is compulsory and imposed. In this view, the meaning of a behavior is not given once and for all. There are a number of stories, calls, and challenges coming from different human sources, into which an individual's own story will be interwoven. What we do with our lives will provide stories that have something in common with other stories. Compulsory

morals, on the other hand, consider that there is one normative story for everybody and impose it on other human stories. In the specific example of human love, compulsory
morals would say that perfect love is a standard for all human beings. A calling ethics, on the other hand, would speak
of a variety of interpretations of love within which my human relationships will find meanings. Calling ethics in no
way shows unconcern with respect to ethical choices, because it emphasizes that the story of each person's existence
will be different according to his choice of action, and that
difference will be irreversible and quite independent of his
good intentions. Each person's story will be "read" by others,
within the context of other possible stories and with a meaning not determined by what the person intended his actions
to do and to communicate. Here we perceive a sort of objectivity of morals. In the end, people will be what they have
made themselves—and this may indeed be the sanction of
the action: whatever I do, I shall forever be someone who did
those things. My actions irreversibly write my story.

We must not confuse calling ethics with the modern liberal idea of tolerance and so-called non-directivity. Indeed,
every statement is a confrontation and an intrusion. It is also
an aggression, in that it irremediably changes its hearers in
some way and causes them to change their idea of the world.
Words may bring peace, but they also bring the sword and
divisions. A calling ethics does not aim at a society in which,
through tolerance and harmony, everybody will be nice and
kind. It tries to talk about a way of living human relations
that, while facing conflicts and struggles, recognizes in other
people human beings who are free and unique. Although it
expressly refuses the domination subtly hidden in obligatory
morality, it denies neither the divergences nor the radical
challenges that may come from others, nor the conflicts, tensions, and existential anguish that accompany these divergences and challenges.

### An example: Christian ethics

In order to understand such perspectives, the example of Christian ethics may be helpful. Christian ethics is considered by some people to be a normative, obligatory morality, whereas for others it works as a calling ethics. For the former, there is an image of what a "good Christian" is, and this image is normative. To be a good Christian, one must follow a whole set of norms. However, it should be noted that the common image of the "good Christian" is often confused—as if by chance—with the image that the dominant group has of itself. For all practical purposes, for many Americans, this image of the "good Christian" has become confused with that of the perfect middle-class American.

Christian ethics can work in a completely different way, starting with the account of the life of Jesus. That life challenges people; it does not tell anyone what must be done, but it opens up a whole dimension of meaning; the story of my existence could follow that of the life of Christ. I can read my life in the light of his poem. One evening at supper with his friends, Jesus said, "Here is my body, here is my life given for you"; challenged by his story and his life, I could share my life. His story can be for me a challenge and a call. Because of his story, it is difficult to look at life without considering that possibility. Christ is not seen as an example, as is the case in the idealistic point of view of an obligatory morality; he is not an abstract and impersonal ideal. On the contrary, a Christian calling ethics speaks of a confrontation with a person who lived in a given social and historical context; this is what the Christian theologian calls the Incarnation. This person gives a singularly positive testimony in his story. From this point of view, Christian ethics no longer appears as a timeless code, but as a confrontation with this historical Jesus. It speaks of the possibility of "rereading" Jesus's "poem" to narrate and incarnate our life through his. In theological terms, Christian ethics traditionally speaks of the possibility of reliving the mysteries of the life of Jesus, and, seen from that angle, it is not an obligatory morality.

### The categories of good and evil

Our thoughts about obligatory morality and a calling ethics lead us to question the notions of good and evil, right and wrong. Is there any meaning to the defining of every action in terms of two categories, one called "right" and the other called "wrong"? Does it make sense to wonder, before performing an action, "Is it right or wrong?"

Before answering these questions, we should point out that our reply refers to the "thought-out" uses of these categories, and not to the more or less spontaneous application of them. In other words, if someone says "It is wrong to kill my neighbor," the person probably does not intend to work out a whole theory of good and evil. He is simply stating his feelings and existential choices, which could be outrage at the idea and rejection of murder as a solution. In everyday use, the categories of right and wrong are often shortcuts used to express quickly a feeling and a choice that would otherwise be difficult to express.

Many people consider that all behavior can be described as right or wrong. In extreme cases, they even go so far as to make such descriptions into objective categories of good and evil. The aim of morals in life then becomes always doing right according to the operative categories and being careful never to deviate from this standard. This approach should be questioned. First, it presupposes a description for every actual form of behavior, and this description is normative. Our analysis concerning the origins of normative notions can be helpful here. In a given society, what is the source of normative ideas? In general, they reflect the dominant ideologies.

The categories of right and wrong seem to function as

ideologies according to the following pattern: anyone who wonders whether an action is good or bad refers to a system of abstract thought on which the judgment is then based. This system of abstract thought, which is the product of the culture, provides standards for actions. In such a perspective, interplay between human beings becomes secondary to the mere confrontation of abstract ideas. Conflicts between people, which underlie ethics, are thus masked. And since the dominant ideology controls the abstract system of ethics, this system of right and wrong is like a trick played by the dominant ideology. Instead of being clearly confronted by the standards that the social organization, and particularly its dominant groups, produce, individuals are confronted by a "good" that seems greater than society. That "good," however, remains always the "good" as perceived by some social groups.

This ideological game can easily be analyzed through a simple example, such as adultery. If one says, "Adultery is wrong," one is faced with an abstract standard that dictates that the act should be avoided. But this abstract presentation hides questions related to criteria and people; according to what criteria, and especially in relation to whom, is one reacting? The attitude would be quite different if the conflicts inherent in the ethical discussion were recognized. Adultery would then be seen, not in its abstract reality, but in the center of an interpersonal network—where its place really is. It would then be possible to listen to what the people involved are seeking. One member of a married couple might say: "Adultery, in my opinion, might destroy the plans we have made together," or, "Adultery would create a conflict between us if it represented a desire to stop building our lives together," or, more plainly still, "If you commit adultery, you will suffer the consequences."

When ethical considerations are made in the context of relationships, the individuals and groups involved—and sometimes conflicting—remain present. The contrary is true, however, when the concepts of "right" and "wrong" are used, because they camouflage personal involvement through their general language. They use a language arising from a so-called neutral point of view, or arising from nowhere in particular.

The way these categories are used, however, reflects an important process in society. People do not communicate directly, but rather through the media of languages and abstractions. In addition, it is never possible to be completely sure who (individuals or social classes or groups) is speaking through the norms that permeate society. As long as languages, abstractions, and norms carry elements that express, structure, and order ethical language, the impersonal categories of right and wrong are a fairly appropriate designation of it.

### A relational viewpoint

The use of these categories of right and wrong, then, creates two problems. First, in concrete terms, the definitions of what is right and what is wrong are usually determined by the dominant ideologies of a given culture. Second, these definitions hide the underlying conflicts. Because of this, individuals are no longer confronted directly by either the dominant groups or by each other, but only by an abstract ideological system.

Considered from another perspective, the meaning of behavior can be approached through relational categories. From this viewpoint, the point of departure in ethical discussion is the question of how to tell the story of one's life. Through their actions, people write their own stories within the social fabric, and others read each story in their own ways. Furthermore, each person can express an opinion as to whether or not the other people's stories accord with his or her own story. It is not a matter of comparing another's story with abstract norms, but of saying to what extent one is ready to assimilate one's own story with that of others. Nor is it an intellectual agreement; it is a practical acceptance with a personal commitment. We often express such a commitment in everyday language by such statements as "I think that's right," or, "In my opinion, that's wrong." Sometimes, divergent and conflicting life projects are thus expressed and confronted. In these relational categories, right and wrong appear as life scenarios with which I do or do not wish to compare my own, and not as general concepts. It is not because something is bad that I do not want it; rather, I label as "bad" what I do not want. Spinoza was thinking along similar lines when he wrote, "We do not follow a course of action because it is right, but on the contrary it is right because we want it."[2] Contrary to idealistic categories, right and wrong in this case are linked to people's concrete undertakings. This relational definition of the meaning of behavior also includes the category of risk. Indeed, one no longer refers to abstract structures, but ventures one's existence without the "cover" or "legitimization" that can assure us in advance that the risk is a "good" one. Faced with a whole series of possible scenarios, we must incorporate our existence into one of them. There is no escape from choice and from risking one's life.

Moreover, it is perhaps to this experience that theories of human freedom refer. They speak of situations in which human beings are led to say to other human beings, "This is the scenario that I wish to insert in the social fabric," or, more precisely, "This is what the individual and social body of my action will be like and, once it has been 'written' in the

2. That does not mean that we want it arbitrarily.

world, it will no longer belong to me. It will henceforth be outside of me in an otherness from which I shall never be able to retrieve it."

We can see clearly from this the ambiguity of the concepts of right and wrong. As idealistic categories, all they do is conceal the standards of the dominant ideologies and the contradictions or conflicts of society. As concepts linked to the concrete experience of human beings, they show where different people situate the risks of their existence and their choices out of the possibilities open to them.

How these categories are used also depends on each individual's social situation. People who feel solidarity with the dominant groups will normally express the meaning of their acts in idealistic terms, thus masking the underlying conflict in their domination. On the other hand, the dominated groups (to the extent to which they have not been taken in by ideological domination) will tend rather to perceive the underlying conflicts directly. In terms of the master-slave dialectic, the master, to justify his position, will call upon legitimizing abstract notions, whereas the slave will speak more simply of the concrete choices in his existence. In more concrete terms, the good ladies discussing a robbery over a cup of tea will say, "Oh dear, isn't it wicked!" while the worker will usually have a more direct reaction, such as, "I am ready to defend what I own against anybody who wants to take it from me." On the one hand, the conflict is concealed by a reference to abstract categories, while on the other hand the conflict is readily apparent. In the same way, we shall find very different attitudes toward prison. In the idealistic categories, the concepts of right and wrong legitimize prison; convicts are said to have done wrong and they are punished for it. In relational categories, one can say more simply that society (or at least its dominant group) defends itself! All together, the categories of good and evil seem to function most

of the time as abstract ideologies that conceal concrete societal or relational conflicts.

### Are morals objective?

The question, "Are morals objective?" is often raised by
critical consideration of the categories of right and wrong, or
of the norms presented in a society. It is usually raised in
such forms as these: "But, after all, can we or can we not say,
once and for all, that such and such a behavior is good or
bad? Is there no way of giving an ethical description to actions independently of people?" Or else, and this is quite different: "Can I, and I alone, decide what is good for me and
thus follow my conscience?" Then some people panic and
ask what would happen if everybody started making their
own moral standards for their actions. "Isn't there any objectivity in ethics then? Is it purely subjective?"

In this section, I shall try to show in what ways ethics
seems not to be objective, and then how the claim to objectivity seems to grasp an important reality.

First of all, I do not think that ethics are objective if by
objective we mean that it makes it possible to describe any
(or even certain types of) behavior as good or bad, based on
criteria that are independant of any individual or collective
bias. To believe that behavior can be classified in this way is
to believe that it can be "read" outside any frame of reference. It is to believe that behavior exists with an identity outside all the concrete social patterns that enable people to
construct their behavior. Elements of behavior, just like what
we call "facts," are social constructs created to give some
shape to a world that would otherwise remain shapeless. In
addition, stating that elements of behavior can be classified
objectively means forgetting the way in which values depend on cultures. It also means neglecting the fact that this

classification is carried out by someone whose vision is determined by a particular social and personal standpoint. In extreme cases, any classification that claims to be universal is just a reflection of an attempt to dominate by people who want their system of thought and values to rule over others. Such domination is indeed actually exercised; witness all the ethical systems whose values appear blatant in historical perspective, but which seemed in their time to be objective and universal. Unless I believe that my reasoning includes absolute truth (and would that not be making an idol of my own reasoning?), I must recognize that my vision is my own and that it is related to the material, intellectual, and social conditions of my perception. In this light, it makes sense to share our meanings, our calls, and the standards that we have adopted. However, to present my (or my group's or my social class's) reading of meanings as the reading of meanings implies that I am setting up an ideological domination by which I would impose on others my particular standards. For some people, moreover, one value is to refuse to impose their rules on others. Certain religious traditions show that they have understood this when they attach to God alone— that is, to the total, intangible Otherness—the absolute meaning of our behavior.

Does this mean, then, that all that counts are our intentions and how we decide to read our behavior? Is there no meaning to the statement that ethical meanings are objective? Is there no sense to the whole of the moralists' tradition of stating that morals are objective? Most traditions stress the fact that moral activity does not only concern intentions or subjectivity; it is part of the tissue of society and by that fact has some independence of all intentions. Whatever I may think, if I shoot a bullet into somebody's heart, that person will be killed. To that extent, ethics are related to a real objectivity. People's actions have their results, which shape the world. Although actions may be interpreted in many different ways, they do not depend solely on the subjectivity of the agent and the agent's own reading. This was one of the contributions of sociologists, who stressed that what some social agents read in one way, others may read differently. Our performances become a *text*, in that they are written once and for all, and this text can be read by others. Sometimes one becomes aware that an action communicates something quite different from what one wanted to say in it. That is why some people can read their activity as action for greater social justice while others, on the contrary, interpret it as paternalism or even as a concrete defense of the interests of the dominant groups. To this extent, morals are objective. The possible readings of our actions are not determined by our intentions. In the field of both individual and collective relations, our acts are also part of a context, which makes it impossible to interpret them in an entirely arbitrary manner. The "texts" of our acts, like literary texts, have their meaning partially determined by context. The stands we take by our concrete solidarities write a "social text" that remains independent of our intentions. To that extent morals are objective, even if there are several "readings" of the acts concerned.

To summarize, the question of objectivity in ethical discourse or morals can be approached in two ways. The first way presupposes that there is a moral standard that instructs us as to what should be done. In this case, objectivity in morals would imply believing that there can be a more or less absolute set of ethics and one single reading of reality. This view turns relative ethical choices into absolutes and neglects the real economic, political, and ideological conditions that affect the creation of ethics. The second way considers ethical behavior objective insofar as people's actions write into the social context a text whose meanings are independent of the intentions of the agents. It insists on objectivity in morals, against those who tend to consider either that it is the intention that counts or that the *right* way of reading their actions is *their* way. This approach stresses the enormous gap between what one thinks one is doing and what one actually does.

Concrete examples of both individual and collective ethics could be helpful here. A pair of lovers may have a perfectly positive reading of their relationship, and therefore consider subjectively that it is something that corresponds to their values. At the same time, others may read their love in a completely different way; for example, that the couple is about to bring a child into the world without being sure of being able to provide it with the necessary conditions for its education; or, their relatives may think that one of the lovers is the slave of other. Whatever good intentions the couple may have and however deep their conviction may be, their actions affect the world, society, and the others around them. Whatever the couple's intentions may be, if a child is born, its life will have an objective reality of its own beyond their intentions. If the only meaning given to the relationship is the reading of the lovers, we have a "lack of objectivity."

Similar situations also arise in collective situations. The case of nineteenth-century Christian missionaries is well known; subjectively, they read their actions as evangelization, while others saw in their efforts the ideological spearhead of colonization. Here again, any analysis limited to the missionaries' frame of reference would seriously lack "objectivity." It is, moreover, paradoxical to note that those who speak most of "objectivity" in the first sense of the word (as absolute standards) often make the least "objective" (in the second sense) analyses of their own actions. This is only to be expected, because the first type of objectivity is often the result of a particular reading considered as an absolute one. Often these "absolute standards" are the expression of the reading of dominant groups that are not too interested in being challenged by more precise analyses.

We should point out that both ways of considering moral objectivity can be found in Max Weber's categories of "morals of conviction" and "morals of responsibility." Morals of conviction emphasize consistency between moral actions and one's principles. These principles are often considered as objective in the first meaning of the word. Morals of responsibility, on the other hand, concentrate on the concrete result of actions (that is, in the words we have been using, the reading made of them in the social context). Morals of responsibility imply that what is important is to act in such a way that one expects to be able to accept responsibility for one's actions. They thus emphasize "objectivity" in our second sense of the word, since the results of actions are analyzed through the different readings of their effects. Missionaries, who acted according to their convictions without foreseeing the consequences of their actions in colonialist terms, acted according to ethics of conviction; they probably believed in the objectivity of ethics according to the first meaning. On the other hand, those who follow an ethics of responsibility accept differences of interpretation of their actions. They believe in moral objectivity in the second sense, and accept that what is achieved is not a necessary outcome of their intentions or convictions.[3]

## The ethical dimension as a form and not as a norm

We answered the question, "Are there universal morals?" by saying that the moral standards that we know are always linked to particular societies and cultures, and especially to the dominant ideologies in the societies. We also pointed out how the notions of right and wrong are usually used to hide conflicts. But the question of what is right could

3. I will comment further on this distinction of Max Weber's in the section on structural ethics.

be put at another level: if no concrete standard can be presented as an absolute, and if judgments stating that certain types of behavior are good and others bad only serve to hide conflicts, would it not be possible to offer ethical requirements as a form of human existence, a form that opens out onto universality? This would seem to be Kant's insight when he stresses that at the root of ethical statements lies a categorical necessity; human beings see their actions through universals of good, of duty, and so forth. Kant does not mean that there are particular norms with their own content; rather, he recognizes that any action raises the question of its meaning in the context of a freedom that determines itself irreversibly.

For some people, Kantian ethics are a matter of requirements and universal principles reflecting the social structures.[4] In their view, each human being hears the voice of conscience calling him or her to "duty," which is usually expressed in specific social norms. This, then, would be another way of promoting the social commandments by linking them to the process of internalization into the superego. Presented in this way, right and duty can no doubt be read as an internalization of social domination. In that case, they would be a false universalization.

There is, however, another way of perceiving Kantian ethics. Human freedom, as its own standard, commits the person irreversibly, and is not perceived in any other way than as realizing its own future. Seen in this light, the ethical dimension of action is to become aware that one is acting in relation to this future. Ethical action is not motivated by any particular reason; all rational explanations are false to a cer-

4. This is probably the case with Kohlberg's ethics, which places the highest degree of ethical development in choices made in the face of abstract and general principles. That is very different from an ethics confronting people with people in conflicting situations.

tain extent, and in any case they are never the ultimate motivation of an action. Ethical action thus is characterized by how people accept being irreversibly involved in a decision. This would seem to be what Kant meant when he presented the categorical imperative in the following maxim: "Ask yourself whether you could regard the action which you propose to do as a possible object of your will if it were to take place according to the law of nature in a system of nature of which you were yourself a part";[5] or, again: "Act as if the maxim of your action were to become, through your will, a Universal Law of Nature."[6] In other words, the categorical imperative says that we are faced with our own will, which becomes part of the world with the implacable irreversibility that the eighteenth century translated by the term Universal Law of Nature. It roughly means: "Assume your will and its consequences."

Understood in this way, the ethical dimension joins Nietzsche's idea that, beyond reason, science, morals, and religions, human beings are confronted with their will. Therefore, the universality of ethics is related, not to the content of a universal moral law, but to the process of freedom that commits itself. The ethical dimension of a concrete action does not come from particular moral codes or subjective motivations, but from this reference to the future that is constructed through the individual will. Perhaps it is in this sense that one should understand the notion of "Duty," so dear to the nineteenth century. Quite apart from all the ways in which it was used ideologically to justify submission to social standards, it undoubtedly reflected the deep insight of human beings who feel confronted by their future. This also

5. Immanuel Kant, *Kant's Critique of Practical Reason and Other Works on the Theory of Ethics*, tr. T. K. Abbot (London, 1909), p. 161.

6. Ibid., p. 38.

means that liberty is never a means (and certainly not a means for obtaining a moral or good universe), but always an end: "So act in such a way that you treat humanity, whether in your own person or in that of any other, as an end, always at the same time never merely as a means."[7] (Note that this last sentence could be construed as a new, subtle way of introducing a standard presented as universal. This is not so if it is understood that this statement is only a reaffirmation of the categorical imperative. It is our action that is involved, and that is not a means.)

From a religious point of view, such a conception of liberty and ethics implies, for the believer, representing God as one who creates humans in freedom, and truly entrusts them with their own history, with all the risks that that means for God. It implies an image of God in which God created human beings for their own sake. For some people, this is what is meant by saying that God created people out of love.

### Ethical involvement beyond critical thought

The analyses that we have presented lead us to see that it is impossible to act without taking, in the end, the risk of one's action in society and in the world, with a limited perception of these. This brings out the relative nature of all ethical involvement. This relativity does not, however, imply moral indifference. Despite the plurality of readings, we are in a given society, with its set of stories and symbols. Whatever critical details we want to express, we are always dependent on our symbolic and linguistic universe. To this extent critical thought has its limits; having recognized the relative nature of all positions, one must nevertheless act. Even not to decide is to decide. There is always a moment—

7. Ibid., p. 47.

called the moment of risk or the moment of trust—at which involvement is based not on critical thought but rather on an intuitive insight that one has not yet learned to comprehend rationally.

To this extent, there is no radical difference between the philosopher and the laborer or farmer, between the religion of the theologian and popular religion. In the end, any action requires trust in the symbolic universe.[8]

Critical thought, therefore, is a relative failure when it comes to trying to explain once and for all the inner meaning of our decisions. Whatever suspicion one casts on our motivations, whatever ideologies are unmasked, whatever mythologies are "demystified," we are only remystifying, restating ideologies, and rationalizing our behavior in new ways. This does not mean that critical thought is useless. Indeed, it assists us in going beyond a naive and unthinking mode of life. However, unless we give up acting, in the end we have to trust the symbolic universe that bears us and our history. Without this radical trust, critical thought seems in the end to be sterile.

Some people, having discovered the limits of thought, want to stop all critical activity and accept totally the symbols of the society in which they live. Their attitude seems to me to be positive, in that it shows the desire to live and to go beyond sterile criticism. It also shows a rejection of that weariness that overtakes those who, without daring to get involved, are, like Hamlet, forever going back over the relative nature of any involvement. Those who choose to stop criticizing and doubting want to accept their lives and their societies. They want to cease remaining outside their world. But this acceptance is not without its difficulties. If, as is often the case, the upper middle classes are caught in a sort

---

8. By "symbolic universe," I mean that the world and the meanings that surround us are marked by the events of our individual and collective history.

of malaise—a total, sterilizing feeling of relativity—the blind acceptance of the world and society is just as barren as the critical activity that it reacts against. The refusal to be aware of the contradictions present in the society (whether they are called *dominations* or *original sin*) is the basis of all fascism. Indeed, this blind acceptance of everything symbolic in a society, which itself is perceived as healthy, is characteristic of fascist ideologies. These ideologies invite people, especially young people, to stop thinking critically and to "trust" the symbolism of their culture. The so-called "moral majority" movement espouses this sort of ideology. We know the extreme results, in Nazi Germany and elsewhere. I believe that blind confidence in the "holy technocracy" brings about similar consequences.

A merely critical way of thinking becomes sterile and paralyzing, while blind confidence leads to some kind of fascism. Is there any other possibility? I think the solution may lie in critical thought accompanied by a certain trust in action. Confident involvement overcomes the paralyzing effect of criticism, while reflection mitigates blind involvement. Philosophies that stress the complementary nature of practice and theory seem to me to follow this approach. Underlying such a position, there is a kind of faith and a kind of hope that are not justified at all by criticism. At the basis of such an attitude is a way of seeing existence in which one feels both its limits (the experience of death) and its possibilities (resurrection). That is why I believe that it is not possible to do without the mystical dimension, where people really commit themselves. Nothing can be proven theoretically about this, but it is a fact that human beings experience in their concrete commitment both their limits and their possibilities.

### Remarks concerning absolute
### ethical maxims

I have tried to show why I do not think it is possible to present ethics as universal and absolute; an ethical system always depends on the sociohistorical context that produced it. However, we must take into account the fact that certain norms have been expressed and are expressed as absolutes; they sometimes seem to convey the best in the ethical tradition of a period. For example, we hear people say, "Whatever motives are given, torture is immoral," or, "Abortion is never permissible," or, "Atomic weapons should be banned in the name of morality." Such moral maxims seem to correspond to something that is very important to people, which they express through moral absolutes that should never be transgressed. What do these statements represent?

In some cases, these maxims appear to be the result of a process that has presented unduly particular ethical positions as an absolute. A serious critical attitude therefore leads one to question the claim that they are moral absolutes. Thus, if the absolute rejection of atomic weapons, torture, abortion, seem to be very respectable ethical positions, it nevertheless is difficult for me to support such positions when people raise them to the level of universality. Without very special understanding, it would seem rather arrogant to offer such simple (if not simplistic) maxims as universally valid for ethical questions about which most people, when confronted with them in real situations, have hesitations.

These absolutist maxims may, however, have a totally different significance. Thus, if people state that, for them, it is imperative to abolish torture, they may simply be indicating where they draw a line concerning acceptable behavior. By drawing such a line, they are personally introducing a strong moral limit that shows their position concerning humanity. Under analysis, the delimitations of any proscription can always be criticized; it is partly arbitrary and is certainly conditioned by sociohistorical elements. One could argue, for example, and ask how torture is defined. Does it include psychological torture, or only physical torture? And in this way the relative nature of the maxim is quickly revealed. But I think that such criticisms neglect one central element: a limit has been expressed. Thus, in a given historical situation, faced with a particular type of torture, the affirmation by someone that torture is completely inadmissible under any circumstances may be of great significance within that particular context. In this case, it is not so much the affirmation of a timeless, universal norm as the practical affirmation of a limit that must be drawn somewhere at a particular point in history. It therefore expresses a definite undertaking with a place in time and in a society and, moreover, belonging to those who associate themselves with it. Taken out of such a context, the stated norms lose their significance. Considering them as a theoretical, ethical statement would be to read them out of context and thus deform them.

Seen in this way, such uncompromising maxims seem to me to be very important; they show where individuals and groups draw moral limits in their analyses. As indicated above, these boundaries are always, in the final analysis, as obscure and partly arbitrary as any taboo. They are the result of decisions rather than of analyses. Finally, we should point out that such ethical statements find their strength less in the normative content that they offer than in the concrete personal *No* with which they confront intolerable situations. In my opinion, such maxims are concrete undertakings linked to precise situations; in this way, they are not to be identified with the general invocation of taboos. Ethical statements made by those personally involved in particular situations can be differentiated from ideological norms, which motivate and legitimate grounds for certain practices, and which by their universalist expression conceal the conflicts present in the situations to which they refer. Thus, the statement "torture is unacceptable" can be, in my opinion, the non-ideological expression of a commitment insofar as it defines somebody's position. But if it claims to solve without being "involved," by using universalist and theoretical arguments (the conflict between those who refuse torture as an instrument and those who accept it under certain circumstances), then this statement becomes part of an ideology that, in fact, only hides the conflict. The same arguments apply to the other examples given, atomic weapons and abortion.[9]

Before concluding this section on general maxims, we should remember that some of them can be analyzed within what I called above the mytho-poetic language. Indeed, such maxims as "One must always love one's neighbor," "One must do what is right," "One must be honest," in contrast to "Thou shalt not torture anyone," have no direct, concrete content. They act as general directives or as a mytho-poetic language to which one can have recourse for analyzing ideologies or practices. It is also in this sense that one can take those moral maxims that indicate general directions without giving concrete mediation. Thus, the statement that one cannot ignore the source of money used in business does not give any concrete indication of what to do in a given situation. And yet the statement of such general standards opens the way to many analyses and critical practices. For exam-

9. Or still others: violence, the death penalty, etc. It is, perhaps, also from this point of view that the real value of Jesus's position in the face of a society in which a woman can be rejected like an object is best seen: "What God hath united, let no man put asunder." Other general statements can also be understood in this light, such as: "Do not confuse politics and religion," "Science is autonomous with respect to its applications," etc. As general statements, they act as ideologies, but in concrete affirmations they also act as taboos, drawing distinctions and lines of demarcation that structure that society. The social construction of reality is always based on such structuring taboos.

ple, it is in the name of such a principle that economic relationships based on exploitation or on apartheid can little by little be called into question. Proclamations of human rights have similar effects. These general principles should not, therefore, be considered as definite norms, but as mythopoetic affirmations that can, in the long run, be of great importance to a society.

### Ethics as an intellectual discipline?

All this leads to questions. What is the meaning of ethics as an intellectual discipline? Is ethics more than a part of the many ideological struggles in a society? Can ethics determine what is right and what is wrong?

If, by such a discipline, some hope to find any kind of neutral forum or knowledge that could come to some conclusion beyond partial and partisan ethical stands, I believe that they are deluded. Ethical discourse seems to me another form of ideology, and each time it presents itself as universal, as in saying that something is absolutely "right" or "wrong," it conceals the individuals or the groups who took the particular stand. I believe it would be more correct to recognize the particular social origin of every ethical discourse, and to say that particular people or groups are for (or against) such or such practices; it is their particular human stand. To say in a general way that something is right is a way to hide the particularity of the position. But the tendency is great to make oneself and others believe that there is a way of presenting a general ethical judgment. It seems to be so much more acceptable, and the personal risk one takes is less felt. When people yield to that temptation, they give up that old wisdom of the Christian tradition, which states that, before the end of time, it is impossible to definitely separate the wheat from the weeds!

Despite these limits, ethics as an intellectual discipline

can be defined. Indeed, it happens that some members of a society conduct a dialogue—either individually or in groups—about their stands and about the reasons they give to explain and legitimize their choices. Through such dialogue, partial, provisionary agreements can sometimes occur. These are then often presented in the form of ethical statements of right or wrong. These agreements can be helpful for individual and social growth. They call or challenge individuals and groups. They clarify certain issues.

It can be useful to institutionalize that kind of dialogue. Through such an informal institution, an intellectual discipline called ethics comes into existence. However, the so-called "ethical statements" remain in the end the ideological statements of the group that produced them. The apparent privilege given to these ethical statements appears, from this point of view, as just another way of concealing which social groups produced them. That is why, most of the time, the intellectual discipline called "ethics" ends by promoting either the dominant ideologies or those of the intellectual middle class.

Often a particular situation becomes an ethical issue thanks to a new awareness of some oppression or conflict. The process usually starts with the suffering and the cries of the oppressed. But because they are oppressed, the poor are often unable to articulate their claim in a way that will be heard. To be oppressed, indeed, means to lack articulate language and power of persuasion. That is where prophetic voices carry much weight. Prophets often are people who, despite being rather privileged and thus possessing some intellectual and social power, choose to be in solidarity with the oppressed. Generally, in the beginning, they are not listened to. But, after some time and some societal evolution of conditions (often including a modification in the relative strength and interests of the groups and individuals involved), others begin to join the prophets and to see why they act as they do. The situation has then become an ethical issue.

Such a process can be observed in many cases. When slavery is considered, for instance, the three steps I described can be discerned. In the beginning, the cries and the suffering were almost not noticed; the poor do not have their history recorded. It is only recently, through the famous book and television program *Roots*, that Americans became generally aware of some history of slavery. In this case, one could say that the prophetic group was primarily the Quakers, joined later by others. And then, slavery became slowly an ethical issue. But that happened in the North first, where the economic conditions "helped" the conscience of the industralized part of the country. Some similar analyses could be worked out for the birth of other ethical issues, such as racism, exploitation, torture, the Vietnam War, sexism, and so forth. It is through these concrete historical struggles that the discipline called "ethics" gradually gets developed in a society. Obviously, ethics does not offer any pat answers to messy ethical problems.

### Conclusions: the positive nature of commitment

It seems impossible, through abstract reflection, to determine right and wrong. In front of commitment—as in front of death—the human being is, to a certain extent, alone. But one question remains: Why do human beings long for liberation? Why do some people feel at one with the poor and the oppressed?

Although history goes on against a background of domination and oppression, it cannot be reduced to only that. It also has the positive aspect of human liberation. I have already mentioned this when introducing the concept of calling ethics: through their actions and their words, human beings have offered calls to other human beings. But these possibilities remain abstract until one becomes involved in them. Before this, they just appear as risks, with the danger that one might get lost in them. However, through human history runs unceasingly the warning that anyone who is afraid of losing his life will really lose it. However great the desire to be sure of one's path, reflection will never anticipate commitment; the final name for commitment is always Trust.[10] But, beyond this loss of self in trust, history resounds with a promise, which is shown by the tenderness of human encounter and reconciliation beyond domination and oppression.

10. Blondel described this limit that thought can never cross very well in his *L'Action* (1893) (Paris: Presses Universitaires de France, 1950). In his *Logique de la vie morale*, he also showed that it was only after a commitment that the principle of contradiction became a force in history (*Premiers ecrits* [Paris: Presses Universitaires de France, 1950]).

# PART TWO

# 6

# INDIVIDUAL AND
# INTERPERSONAL ETHICS

## Guidelines for individual ethics

In this chapter, I will present some grounds for an individual ethics. It must be clear that mine is only one approach among many. One presupposition of my approach is a reading of human relations that recognizes that they are built around relations of domination. It could be submitted that this same basic reading is to be found in Christian traditions that speak of original sin. In order to understand the implications of what I present here, we will have to consider the social environment that is congenial to such an ethical approach. Then, we will have to examine the limitations of any individual ethics. A second presupposition will be that individual ethics are complementary to a more collective dimension, which I shall call structural ethics. Finally, I shall show how all these ethical statements are rooted in culture, with central and peripheral elements. It is on such a basis that we shall then sketch out guidelines for individual ethics.

### Social context of ethics

By stating that relations of domination lie at the heart of human relationships, I mean that, given the historical evolution of society, all human beings are caught up in a history in which certain people are oppressed and exploited. I mean that relations of domination put a burden on the lives of all people, either because they are oppressed or else because they are alienated in and by the defense of their privileges. Such a perspective implies a certain distance from those who believe that individuals can do what they want with their existence. With respect to this last issue, two basic hypotheses confront each other in society. One ideology, centered on the concept of free enterprise and the puritan work ethic, says that it is possible for everyone to "make it" as long as they "try hard enough." This same ideology presents competition in society, in school, and in industry as fair and healthy. The other ideology, by contrast, starts from a reading of society that stresses the structures of domination, as well as the impossibility of any individual completely escaping social alienation.

The basic hypothesis of the myth of equality is that everything is still possible for the newly born human being. Bright prospects for achieving one's objectives in *society-as-it-is* are held out before each individual; any obstacles are supposed to come from individual limitations. As long as one is normally gifted and willing to work and take initiatives, the sky is the limit. This presupposes that history has only a superficial effect on people, since the social, economic, and cultural conditions in which a child is born are considered to have very minor importance. Everybody's chances at school are said to be equal, and so on through life.

Everyone can "make it" by their own effort. Conflicts arising in one's existence, especially structural interest conflicts, are concealed by the ideology of harmony and tolerance; within the myth of equality, competition is always said to be fair and based on equal opportunity.

Exactly opposite presuppositions underlie the view of the world that is the background of my ethical thesis. My fundamental hypothesis is that history influences individuals in their innermost selves, in addition to physical and biological limitations, so that everything is not possible for everybody. By the very fact of being members of human society, people suffer from the limitations and harms arising from the past. The human community is seen as a community of oppression, in which people exploit and dominate their fellow human beings. Although there exist many possibilities, individuals are born neither equal nor free in relation to historical conditions. By the very fact of sharing existence in society, everybody is limited and partially paralyzed. These historical limitations are not only external; they also affect the deepest reaches of each person's psychology. This does not deny that the human community also offers possibilities, but it stresses the other aspect; it does not imply, either, that the effects of all limits are negative.

Seen from this point of view, injustices and oppression arise out of a society built on human choices and historical decisions, which are therefore not considered the result of an inexorable destiny. Nobody, today, is individually responsible for the fact that the human community is a community of oppression, but everyone has their share in it and is (objectively if not subjectively) an accomplice in maintaining society's ills. We find ourselves faced with a collective structure, sometimes referred to as collective sin, systemic sin, or even institutionalized evil. This situation stems from human history and human actions, but it does not make any sense to blame any individual for it.

These two viewpoints are linked to very different social positions. The myth of equality and its optimistic view of society show all the characteristics of the ideologies of the dominant groups, who always see the world as being basically well-organized and lacking any insuperable contradictions. This is only to be expected, since it is the dominant groups that have organized the world according to their social position. On the other hand, the recognition of the relationships of domination, based on the hypothesis that society is basically badly organized and oppressive, seems to occur mainly among the poor and the oppressed. From their point of view, the world appears neither harmonious nor well-ordered; it looks badly organized and full of contradictions. Where for the privileged classes everything seems possible for everybody, for the oppressed it is obvious that everybody is affected by the evil in society. Furthermore, the interest the privileged have in concealing the historical origins of their situation is equaled only by the opposite interest of the oppressed. It is therefore as important for the privileged to assert that all people are equal as it is obvious to the oppressed that some are "more equal" than others.

The oppressed and the poor know through their own experience the effects of oppression and exploitation. As they become aware of oppression as the cause of their suffering, they are ready to question societal structures and injustices. They are ready to fight for global, systemic, and structural change. The upper class also recognizes the crucial role of societal organization, and usually wants to defend its dominant position. The middle class, by contrast, feels powerless, but it does not suffer enough from the system to rebel against it. As a consequence, middle-class ethics rarely reaches a global and structural perspective. It accepts society as it is, and limits its scope of inquiry to individual and relational problems. Middle-class people usually consider societal and political issues as too big to confront. They thus stress personal integrity and principles. They emphasize being "nice" and "just" in their immediate neighborhood, while leaving to others the burden of concern for society at large.

The ethical thesis that I will present here presupposes the existence of relations of domination or of original sin. Consequently, my thesis is not universal, but stems from my solidarity with a specific position in society and history: solidarity with the oppressed.

### Individual ethics and structural ethics

My second presupposition is that a useful distinction can be made between two ways of looking at ethical questions: one gives rise to ethics for the individual, and one introduces collective or structural ethics. Two separate and complementary points of view concerning the world correspond to these two ethical perspectives. The first considers social reality as a given fact; the other sees it as something still to be built.

A person in a particular situation, and alone in facing it, can consider that his or her action will scarcely change the framework within which the action will be carried out. A physicist would say that such action is negligible in relation to the statistical set within which it takes place. Such is the case of a woman who is pregnant and wonders whether or not to have an abortion. Although it may be claimed that her decision might influence other people and the collective structures, we can say in general that her decision will have a negligible effect on them. It is first and foremost an individual problem. The same is true of anyone who wonders whether to refuse, individually, to buy goods produced through the oppression of underpaid and exploited workers.

In these and similar situations, the context of the action is given once and for all, and the problem is virtually an individual one. This obviously is a simplified point of view, because there are no purely individual problems; collective problems would not exist without individual problems added together; but it is also true that isolated individual efforts are not enough to change the world.

Within the framework of individual morals, the effects of acts are more or less direct; one individual acts in relation to one or more others. The situation is well defined from the start and will hardly be modified during the action. When structural effects are recognized, one gets a completely different perspective.[1] Some actions, without necessarily having an immediate, precise effect, have repercussions on the way in which the social situation is defined and thus produce a statistical result. If, for example, there is insufficient parking space in a town, the individual approach of not parking there will have very little effect. At the most, someone else will park in the space thus left empty. In the end, the problem will remain the same. But greater efficiency will be obtained if the town, taking the problem from a structural level, sets up parking meters. Nobody will be prevented from parking, but statistics have shown that, by modifying the structure of the problem, results can be obtained. The action of setting up parking meters depends on an analysis of the parking problem in which the initial data on the problem have not been taken for granted. They have been reconsidered from a collective or structural point of view.

Let us take another example, this time from the field of medicine. Ethical problems are raised at the level of the indi-

1. Structural causes are those that cause effects in micro-situations by a statistical action arising from global structures. Thus, increasing the temperature of a gas does not cause any visible movement, but it accelerates certain molecules. In a psychological situation, shutting several people up in a room will eventually arouse arguments, even if no particular cause for discord has been introduced.

vidual. Thus, a doctor may wonder how much money to charge a patient. This is an individual problem insofar as payment is accepted in medicine for each act. But another question, collective and structural, can be raised: Should payment for medicine be worked out in relation to each case? In this view, it is no longer an individual question, but a collective question regarding the whole issue of the organization of medicine.

Another example concerns solidarity among students. According to individual ethics, one would try to promote collaboration among students and an attitude of understanding, while not challenging university structures. Taken from a structural point of view, this problem would call for other actions, such as a reform of university organization so as to give greater recognition to group work and to change the system by which individual examinations alone determine each student's future. The individual point of view presupposes and accepts existing social structures, while a structural action is characterized by the fact that, as a result of an analysis that has discovered how the structures work, it takes structural effects into account.

To understand the difference between the structural approach and the individual one, the example of a group in a vacation place may be helpful. Suppose that the group is full of tensions and life becomes impossible in the house where they are staying. The individual approach would be to examine (perhaps with the help of a psychologist) all the personal problems of each vacationer to find out why relations have gone sour. This approach will usually tend to "moralize" the problem, that is, to suggest personal changes for each individual to bring back harmony. The structural approach would be quite different. It would, for example, start with an analysis stating that disputes resulted from the fact that there was not enough room for everybody, because there were too many people in the house. If this proved to be a structural cause for the arguments (even though a psychological cause for each argument could also be found), the remedy would be to change that structure—in this case, to increase the living space. The structural change is then considered a necessary (if not a sufficient) condition for solving the problem. Furthermore, it would be considered of little help to moralize with the individuals until the structural cause of the problem had been modified.

This example throws a clear light on the debate between advocates of "conversions" and "changes of mentality" as the primary means of solving social problems, and those who consider that structural changes should be tackled first. There are two distinct levels that, to a certain extent, are complementary. The structural approach does not neglect the fact that, in order to change structures, for example, to enlarge the vacation house, individual action is necessary; but it does situate the problem in quite a different way from those who want to act only on individuals and not at all on the structural conditions.

An action is always limited and can only be proposed within the framework of a given society. But an action that presupposes that the structures will always be the same differs from an action of those who can envision change. I therefore use the term structural ethics for reflection that addresses itself to the significance of actions with reference to social systems. This is a complex reflection, because the structural relationship between the acts and their consequences is neither direct nor easy to analyze. In individual morals, there is an obvious correlation between my action and its consequence: If I shoot somebody, I kill that person. But if I buy South African products, the correlation between my gesture and apartheid is much less clear. A detailed analysis of the situation in and the politics of that country is necessary before I can determine the potential meaning of what I do in relation to it.

It is relatively easy to present individual ethics, but much more difficult to present structural ethics. While I will treat structural ethics in greater detail later on, some basic elements must be presented here, in order to situate individual ethics in their collective framework.

Structural ethics always entail an analysis of society, that is, a description of society to be used as a guide for one's actions. This analysis is always limited. Its claim to be "scientific" is often stressed; but if by that we mean that an analysis can be free from the particular conditions in which it is done, we remain prisoners of the myth that science is objective and neutral. However, a precise meaning can be given to the term "scientific analysis": an analysis that, on the one hand, avoids moral exhortations that describe behavior as good or bad, and, on the other hand, avoids empiricism that describes the world without being aware of its own theoretical presuppositions. A scientific social analysis, therefore, takes enough distance from a too subjective view to be aware of cultural biases, as well as of biases linked to class and group interests.

A scientific study always starts from a precise social standpoint. If one accepts, for example, that in a given situation there are dominant and dominated people, it is important to know from which point of view the analysis is to be carried out. Even a structural ethical thesis depends, therefore, on choices that are themselves, finally, impossible to analyze. These are choices of solidarity; they can never be completely justified. Why do people take such and such an option in society? Why, for example, do some people want to be in solidarity with the oppressed, while others do not? Such options imply philosophical reasons, in the broadest sense of the word, or religious ones. Christians, for example, can choose to be on the side of the oppressed because their reading of the Gospels and their study of Jesus Christ's options encourage them in that direction. In other cases, the same solidarity with the oppressed can be founded on quite different reasons than religious ones. However, these pre-analytical choices are usually linked to the ways in which one has already been affected by calls from other individuals and groups already committed within the social texture. They do not arise within the individual alone.

### The sociocultural roots of ethical themes

An ethical statement is always situated within a specific culture and based on choices of solidarity that are just as specific. It is therefore never absolutely new and original. On the contrary, it is the product of a context whose mark and presuppositions it bears. It is determined by a whole series of elements. Moreover, an ethical theme is not produced anywhere or at any time in a society. It arises from the particular questions that certain groups are asking themselves. If all behavior were taken for granted by everybody, no ethical stands would ever be produced. They always arise from some situation where questions are being asked. These questions, in turn, are linked to particular practices; for example, it is during armed conflicts or economic crises that rules of war or social morals are discussed. In the same way, it is when certain medical practices present difficulties that ethical theories on health care are produced. It is also when family and sexual habits are changing that moralists become concerned with them. In each of these cases, concrete situations have led to particular questions. Morals are not deduced from a general view of what humanity is; rather, they stem from precise problems raised by practices that have to be faced. Moreover, we can take the relative abundance of ethical statements about a particular theme as an indication that people are not sure what should be done.

Since ethical questions always arise from somewhere, it does not really make sense to offer global ethical answers with once-and-for-all values. On the contrary, a moral philosophy can only be understood as a particular discourse produced by certain groups or certain people; the practical effect of such discourse is to modify social behavior in one way or another. To that extent, an ethicist acts on society and is an agent for social change or social control.

What I have just said presupposes that no statement is completely independent of the cultural, political, and economic conditions in which it is produced. That is why we believe that it makes little sense to claim that a certain ethical perspective can be detached enough from culture to be an authoritative critic of it. On the contrary, ethics are part of the culture, as a social product. Ethical language would be surpassing its epistemological basis if it were to set itself up as a global censure, with a universal scope capable of judging the society in which it is formed. We must therefore be careful not to confuse the ever-questioning attitude of the moralist who, within a particular culture, challenges a certain number of things, with the abstract point of view of somebody who claims to sit outside the cultural conditions, to watch what happens.[2]

I consider ethical statements, then, not as universal theses, but as particular ways of questioning in which some

2. Here it is important to distinguish the questioning that is inherent in Christian practices from a certain "Christian faith," which claims to judge cultures and societies. It would seem, indeed, correct to say that, within certain Christian practices and the way in which the Christian sets out to follow Jesus Christ, there is a questioning of social practices. This is what I would call the questioning inherent in Christian practices. Christians thus adopt a critical point of view (which discerns, judges, and wonders about the kind of criteria that are used in particular situations). But this does not mean that Christian faith can claim to sit outside a culture and judge it. Such a "faith" would promote a fictitious Absolute, more like an idol. Christianity is not that.

people, individually or in groups, stake their lives as they decide what they want to do and what their solidarity is. In so doing, they question the meaning of their existence.

### Center versus periphery

In general terms, the interpretation of ideological statements and of social practices implies distinguishing the essential from the accessory, the central from the peripheral. For example, in a colonialist social system, the world view puts the "mother country" in the center and the colonies on the periphery. In the same way, we realize when we examine institutions that certain mechanisms are closer to the center of social activity than others. In our Western society, for example, the economic institutions are obviously central. Other institutions and groups remain on the periphery. This is the case in certain communes that aim at restoring the agrarian nature of our society. The distinction between a center and a periphery also has its meaning in ethics. We call the center of ethics those practices that are considered essential to what a statement wishes to legitimize, and the periphery of ethics those elements and values that are considered secondary. For example, if we study the ethical topics produced by the nineteenth-century bourgeoisie, we find sexual practices were considered central, whereas questions of justice were seen as peripheral. Offences against sexual morals were considered very serious, while those against justice were more or less ignored.

This "center versus periphery" distinction requires qualification. What is central in theory can often become peripheral in practice, and vice-versa. In the nineteenth century, for example, sexual ethics were theoretically central, while social ethics appeared to be clearly secondary and peripheral. However, when one looks at the offences that that society tolerated and did not tolerate, we find quite a different system. In practice, it was behavior that challenged the socioeconomic system that really disturbed people. Deviant sexual behavior by members of the male sex was tolerated, as long as such practices did not endanger the family, and especially the production of heirs. What was central, in reality, was perhaps not so much the sexual ethic as such, but the maintenance of a social order. It is therefore useful to distinguish between the theoretical and the real center and periphery. The former concerns the ideological themes that justify social situations; the latter concerns the actual practices of people in that society.

## The ideological function of the center versus periphery distinction

The distinction between the center and the periphery (between what is most important and what is secondary) plays an important ideological role. Indeed, it is necessary to the maintenance of a given social order (and therefore of the dominant groups) that ethics not analyze certain actions too closely. Consequently, through an often unconscious mechanism, ethics concentrates on questions other than those that might disturb practices on which the social order is based. Moral theses, by diverting attention to the peripheral elements of social practices, thus make it possible to conceal problems those practices created. A certain number of sociologists, for example, wonder if the weight given to sexual morals in the nineteenth century did not, among other things, serve to protect the social practices of the industrialist bourgeoisie from the investigations of moralists. As long as morals concentrated on individual practices and scarcely mentioned collective situations, the bourgeoisie could, and in fact did, carry on its economic and social practices with a good conscience. It is therefore not by chance that these practices, which were central to the actual functioning of industrial society, were on the periphery of ethical themes. In this way, bourgeois morals concealed the interests of the dominant groups. In fact, it is not unusual for the officially central ethical concerns to be peripheral to the problems that dominant groups perceive in society.

The distinction between the center and the periphery also enables a society to evolve rather smoothly. Indeed, in the center of the ethical system there is a clear separation between acceptable and non-acceptable behavior. Things on the periphery can be settled by various means, and a certain latitude may be accepted, making it possible to defend a certain "nucleus of essential values" while compromising on elements considered secondary. Changes in these "essential values" can occur when central elements slide towards the periphery. When they are felt to be peripheral, they can be questioned, and changes can be envisaged. However, the strategy of those in power, who wish to preserve the established social order, will be to distinguish the essential from the secondary and prevent such sliding from taking place; they seek to separate the good grain from the tares. Seen in this light, this parable from the Gospels really appears to be subversive. Indeed, although any established order presupposes that it is possible to distinguish what is valid from what is not (the good grain from the tares), the parable declares that human beings will not be able to tell one from the other until the end of time. When, in the parable, the master orders the servants not to pull up the tares in case they also pull up the good grain at the same time, he indicates how impossible it is to distinguish what is central, what is valid, from what is just parasitic. Such language is subversive insofar as it removes a certain number of certainties concerning what is "good" and what is "bad." It prevents the taboos from working.

This distinction between the center and the periphery is useful for analyzing two structural changes in the ethical reading of the world that are presently taking place in the West. These changes concern sex and social justice. Sexual morality, which used to be considered absolutely central, is more and more being considered peripheral, while the opposite shift has occurred regarding social problems. This structural change is probably most visible in Catholic communities. Whereas a few decades ago most Catholics confessed offences against sexual ethics above all others, they seem more likely today to accuse themselves of sins against social justice.

### Tales for individual ethics

Presenting an individual ethical point of view means presenting stories on the basis of which people can tell their own individual story. I shall start by presenting the story of three metamorphoses of the spirit, taken from Nietzsche with a few modifications.

In the beginning, said Zarathustra,[3] the spirit became a camel. The camel can transport heavy burdens for long distances. In this way, the camel, or the human being that it represents, is capable of great sacrifices and extraordinary courage to reach an ideal. As a camel, he submits to all the norms that morals, religion, reason, and science present to him. These authorities legitimate all his actions. The camel never does anything of himself; he checks first to see if the authorities allow him to act, and when these authorities allow him to act, and especially if they order him to do something, then he becomes capable of a great deal. Neither sacrifices nor heroism will be lacking along his path towards the ideal or the holiness that is his aim. He may, moreover, find a real satisfaction in the accomplishment of his duty and the pursuit of his ideal. In Nietzsche's opinion, however, he remains

3. Friedrich Nietzsche, *Thus Spake Zarathustra* (First Discourse of Zarathustra).

always a slave. For example, he is incapable of overriding the orders which are given to him with "reason," or with any other legitimizing authority. For him, all disobedience is wrong. And the idea that he has of himself, that of a being which absolutely must do what is right, means that he is very subject to ideological domination. Producing a slave ethic, the camel is always ready to defend the authorities that, after all, dominate him.

"Then the camel became a lion." The lion rebels, and in so doing he fights the dragon called "Thou shalt." In his rebellion, the lion proclaims his will, but still remains incapable of creating anything. His rebellion remains an empty thing, conditioned by reaction to the camel's submissiveness. In this rebellion, however, he discovers disobedience. It is the stage in which the human being, aware of the limits imposed by the legitimizing authorities, takes the risk of rebelling. He feels aloneness in this experience, because he is no longer protected by the usual legitimating authorities (reason, science, morals, religion). He fights them and unmasks everything false and limited in them. Furthermore, since disobedience is always the act of overstepping an order—be it a logical, rational, scientific, moral, or religious order—it always seems irrational. It is impossible, in fact, to use the rational structures on which one previously depended to support one's action of going beyond the old limits. That is why transgression is usually felt as a risky act as well as an act of trust. In such experiences, people risk their future existence. This transgression is not experienced in the face of abstract ideals of good and ill, which are denounced by the lion, but rather in the face of people and groups with whom one has relations. That is why this stage also leads one to build new relationships. Nietzsche uses the image of the child to symbolize the metamorphosis to which transgression may lead.

"Thus the spirit, after being a lion, became a child." And the child started to laugh, started to play, started being itself and daring to say, without justifying itself, legitimizing itself, or revolting, "This is what I want." To assume peacefully such an attitude (and here we certainly depart somewhat from Nietzsche), the child must trust. Trust enables the child no longer to need to legitimize everything it does. It no longer even needs to say that it is allowed to be a child. It simply exists. It no longer fears taking risks with its life. Seen in this way, the child is simultaneously very much alone and in communication. It is alone because it no longer submits to legitimizing authorities, having left the crowd, which obeys them blindly. But yet it is in communication, because it is only inasmuch as it feels accepted and loved that it can manage to live in its solitude, alone, on its own two feet. For this to happen, I think existence must be structured in a relationship in which one asks for forgiveness, accepts being forgiven, and yet does not make of forgiveness a new kind of legitimization. Indeed, it is because it feels welcome for itself, with its limits and deficiencies (which is what "being forgiven" means), that the child can say quietly, "This is what I want."

The experience of going from being a camel to being a child is sometimes called *liberation*. Through that experience (which, moreover, is always incomplete and in process), persons become free of the need to legitimize their actions all the time. This liberation is gratuitous, a gift, which explains why it does not make sense to say that all human beings must go from the situation of the camel to that of the child. Such a view would purely and simply imply that the journey was a norm, that is, a camel's way of life. Liberation must therefore not be perceived as an obligation, or a task to be achieved, but rather as an event that takes place. The only way to describe it is to say that it occurs gratuitously, that is, without any reason. This view coincides with the Christian language that speaks of salvation through grace, that is, entirely gratuitously. To state that one is gratuitously freed or loved does not in any way deny the fact that the other person is interested in us and finds us important; the interest of the other encourages us.

This of course does not mean that liberation takes place by chance; on the contrary, it takes place thanks to actions within the economic, political, cultural, and individual conditions of the life of each person and group. Thus, access to the stage of the child is perceived as gratuitous by the person who attains it, while under analysis it appears to be the result of actions within the human community. It is therefore non-sense to encourage people to become a "child." Firstly, because trying to become anything may only reinforce camel-like tendencies, and, secondly, telling someone to become as free as a child, to transgress a certain number of oppressive social norms, is inviting them to assume a risk that may not be within their capacities. Presenting it as something normal and normative is to speak like those who dominate their lives. It also means ignoring economic, political, and cultural restraints. And finally, it may mean pushing those who do not feel capable of living more freely deeper into their problems. Nevertheless, it is important that the possibility of living freely, of living as children, should be affirmed and proclaimed. The existence of people who enjoy a certain freedom in fact appears to be for others a challenge and a sign of the possibility of doing likewise. In this sense, it is "good news."

Finally, we should point out that the three stages of camel, lion, and child are always mixed within the individual. Nobody is completely camel or lion or child. At certain moments we are more one than the other, but we are never rigidly in one stage of the metamorphoses.

Nietzsche's story of the three metamorphoses of the

spirit is told so that many people can recognize and recount their own evolution in it. To this extent, we can say that it is a kind of call and a particular ethical theme concerning individual ethics.

## A morality of avowal and pardon

In this presentation of the three metamorphoses of the spirit, we departed somewhat from Nietzsche's point of view by linking the stage of the child to a dynamic of forgiveness. It is perhaps a weakness of the story of the metamorphoses that it portrays the individual as an isolated being and ignores relationships between human beings. This indicates that several stories are necessary to express the many dimensions of human activities. I shall therefore introduce another type of story, in which avowal and forgiveness play a greater part.

We should first of all point out that individual ethics in no way necessarily means individualistic ethics. Individual ethics includes the ethics of relationships, insofar as these relationships are perceived as interpersonal ones, but not as being directly regulated by the collective structures of society.

In the background to this story, which constitutes an ethic of avowal and forgiveness, is the hypothesis of the "wounded" relationship; this may be expressed in terms of oppression, of errors, of sins, of isolation, or of a basic evil. The mythical image that arises is that of the difficulties of communicating and of interpersonal conflict. This background element, moreover, is not definable outside these very stories, which give it its meaning. It presupposes a dimension of violence in all communication, insofar as one imposes one's presence on another and aggresses against the other by what one is.

The story that I am presenting here starts from an awareness of the mistake or of the fault, in order to explore the dimension of forgiveness. The mistake is conceived at first as a blemish, a stain, a weight on one's existence. That is the situation of someone who feels alienated and feels at a distance from the others. The mistake, the impurity, or the crushing taboo are what is felt by anyone who, in someone else's presence, feels isolated and out of communion. At this level, perception agrees with all the mythical stories of impurity; the person feels tainted, rejected, cut off; and yet this situation is not expressed rationally. "Sin," at this level of consciousness, is nothing other than this weight.

In a further stage, the fault can be described rationally; here we speak of transgression. From this point of view, we presuppose an established order within which the state of "sin" is perceived as the transgression. An ethical case can then be argued, because some order (whatever its origins) makes it possible to reason and to say why something is or is not contrary to it. That is the role of ethics, which appears to be both normative and rational.

In the third stage, it is no longer a matter of facing an order or a law, nor of being the subject of a taboo; it is a matter of being face to face with another person. For instance, we stand before someone (an individual or a collectivity) who is crying out because he or she or it is oppressed, crushed, and who awakens a response by that cry. Sometimes it is not the victim but somebody else, such as a prophet, who stands up to express the suffering of the oppressed person or persons. Then the distance, the limitations, and the wound in the relationship will be felt and the cause of isolation from the other or others will be perceived. This is not felt on one's own, or in light of an abstract principle, but rather in a personal encounter.[4] If the other's eyes are sufficiently kind and

---

4. This, of course, is one dimension of the Christian notion of "sin": it is not a transgression, it starts from a relationship. This kind of relational ethics differs drastically from Kohlberg's ethics. For the latter, mature ethical behavior is not to be confronted to people but to universal principles.

welcoming, it is possible to break the isolation and to say something concerning limits and sin. What is then said is called the avowal. It is what I say to the other person to express who I am and at the same time it is a request; a request to be accepted as I am, a request to be forgiven. When a relationship can be lived at this level, the perception of what is wrong is very different from that which occurs when the mistake is experienced as something forbidden or as a transgression. The "sin" is defined as "What I shall mention to explain my request to be accepted as I am." It is only within that request that the fault and the resulting hurt begin to form a real part of the relationship; it then becomes even its flesh and body. It will not be forgotten, but forgiven, which is very different.

In this type of story, the individuals are not considered to be isolated or independent people, finding justification for their lives in their actions or in themselves. On the contrary, existence is considered justified because one at last trusts in being accepted. And, because of one's limitations and mistakes, that acceptance finally always means forgiveness. To paraphrase Louis Lavelle: "Even the errors that others have committed towards us create between us a closer fleshly bond which the forgiveness makes spiritual." Seen in this light, the errors and the limitations are not to be previously eliminated so that a deep relationship can be created. Rather, they are concrete elements in which the relationship nourishes itself and lives through forgiveness. We may even wonder if a relationship that has not yet internalized this dimension of mistake, hurt, avowal, and forgiveness, has not remained very superficial. Until people have felt their respective limits and the wounds that result from them, until they have succeeded in integrating these into their relationship through avowal and forgiveness, they will keep a distance from one another to such an extent that we may well wonder if they really "touch" one another. Forgiveness is the human response to the original violence implied in all relationships.

What I have just said about forgiveness must be carefully distinguished from guilt and imputability. Our culture is so deformed by our concepts of law and justice that it often happens that many people do not think of asking for forgiveness unless they feel they have deliberately done somebody wrong. When forgiveness is experienced in this manner, it is very closely related to law and order, which can determine right and wrong. If one is right, according to this view, there is no sense in asking for forgiveness. But when we consider the avowal process, the point of view is quite different. Asking for forgiveness is the movement by which I leave the isolation to which the violence inherent in any communication has sent me, to open myself out to another, by asking for something from that other person. By so doing I open myself to a relationship of trust and vulnerability. It is, moreover, not so relevant to know whether I am right or wrong—such judgments always depend on the frame of reference chosen or the reasons for relative choices. I ask for forgiveness simply because, in the relationship, the other has been wounded and aggressed upon.[5] That does not mean that the other will not be wounded again; as long as there is a relationship, people are wounded. But it does mean that the parties want this wounded part of the relationship to be lived together, in trust and vulnerability, as a part of a common history.

Some examples might help to clarify this abstract story. Lovers will always wound and aggress against each other. The only way they could avoid it would be to become indifferent to each other and no longer to desire to be loved by each other. Up to a certain point, it is impossible for them to

5. By "aggression" I imply the psychological meaning of "intrusion," not the everyday meaning with its pejorative connotations.

separate what unites them from what wounds them. That is why seeking forgiveness does not necessarily imply that they perceive particular points of behavior they would like to change. And yet they can live their bond as a forgiving relationship, that is, accepting the other's aggression and limitations, and reciprocating the other's request for acceptance—a request that is far from being a demand, since it implies vulnerability.

In the same way, teachers always wound and aggress upon their students in one way or another; this does not mean that teachers should regret behaving as they do, because it would probably be impossible for them to find another way of being that would wound less. In other words, it is meaningful for teachers to ask their pupils' forgiveness, without implying that they feel particularly guilty.

The relationship of forgiveness can thus be envisaged independently of guilt. Contrary to frequent usage, it is possible for people mutually to seek forgiveness without considering the behavior being forgiven as bad. The seeking of forgiveness does not imply a moralizing or judging attitude. It is one dimension of all encounters, insofar as one recognizes that all relationships wound—for reasons that can be described in different ways, such as social alienation, original sin, and so forth. It implies the desire to go beyond the limits of the violence of relationships, while recognizing that this is never completely achieved. Seen in this way, seeking forgiveness does not cause guilt feelings in the morbid sense of the term, but rather opens the relationship through the trust that the other will accept me. This unconditional and total acceptance can sometimes be found in religious language, including Christian faith: God loves us unconditionally; he is a God of forgiveness.

### Justice and love

Another way of telling the story of human relations at the individual level uses the distinction between justice and love. Human beings are both different and in communion. Before living in unity, one must first respect the differences. Stories of justice refer to these differences; they speak of what must be done to respect the others as others.

It would usually be hypocritical to begin a relationship by speaking of friendship. Before I can be friends with the bartender, I must first pay for my glass of beer. Before the lecturer and the student can be friends, they have to situate each other in their respective roles and the conflicts that underlie them. The distinction between love and justice, therefore, gives a structure to certain stories by stressing the fact that one must start by respecting differences before talking of friendship or communion. These stories suggest that the demands of justice (difference) should precede talk of disinterested love. It is only when the difference between individuals has been recognized that one may perhaps talk of love.[6]

This is why the law of justice decides what a just contract should be, in order that a relationship will not become an aggression. It therefore does not directly express the law of love, but is a mediation for it, taking form in written or unwritten laws, depending on the culture and the legal system of the society in which they are produced. It is nevertheless interpreted as an expression of the law of love inasmuch as it is supposed that, to love, one must first respect justice. When these stories speak of justice, they therefore lay down a distinction between love and intrusion. They show the difference between injustice, which confuses love and intrusion,

6. It should be noted that, in this section, the word "justice" is used with a slightly different meaning from that of the chapter on law, where it was used in its juridical sense.

and justice, which seeks to respect this distinction. Rejection of the distinction between love and intrusion can be seen as clearly in a very rigid and global structuring of life as in the absence of any structure. As typical examples, we could mention paternalism, as well as certain "hippy" communes. Paternalism tries to apply the law of love before recognizing the demands of justice; it telescopes the law of justice by claiming to give through love that which should be negotiated through justice. Some hippy communes, by refusing any structure, seek to establish love on spontaneity without prior recognition of the differences between human beings; this sort of destructuring often leads to some people's being crushed because their individuality is not recognized. Sheer spontaneity often opens the way to domination by the strongest.

Finally, this interpretation of justice also reintroduces a certain objectivity into moral action, because the "law of justice" does not depend on intentions or on sincerity. The written and unwritten laws, accepted rules, regular procedures, and all sorts of legitimizing processes are mediations that show us how to respect differences and prevent sincerity from becoming an aggression. If these "laws" are not respected, nobody knows what life in society may bring, and the weakest always suffer.

### The multifarious stories in individual ethics

I have developed some stories or points of view that provide frames of reference and of interpretation of human lives, taken individually or interpersonally. These outlines give a glimpse of how individual ethics can work, but are scarcely even the beginnings of a synthesis on this subject. What has been presented here is often called a "personalist" approach to ethics;[7] it recognizes individuals in their relationships. Personalism certainly expresses great depth in human relationships. A personalist approach, however, differs from personalist ideologies, which remain at the level of individual or interpersonal ethics, without touching the collective structures of society. Sometimes, proponents of this approach claim that human relations include the whole field of ethics; these personalist ideologies, in the end, eliminate collective and structural questions and consider only interpersonal relationships.[8]

7. The "personalist movement," or the philosophy of "personalism," stems from the thought of Emmanuel Mounier, in France, in the 1930's.

8. We must not confuse these "personalist ideologies" with the strong personalist philosophy of Mounier.

# 7

# EMOTIONAL RELATIONSHIPS
# IN A GIVEN SOCIETY

Of all ethical topics, the morality of emotional and sexual relationships holds an important place in our culture. After putting this area of ethics into context, I will approach it in two different ways. First, I will make a necessarily schematic analysis of the way in which sex and the body have been conceived in what I will call traditional society. I will examine in particular the important role sex plays from an economic and political point of view, as well as from a cultural point of view. Secondly, I will try to show possible developments in sexual and relational mores.

This chapter is even more closely bound up than the others with the self-seeking aspects of our society. It is therefore difficult to offer anything other than orientation, with all the vagueness that that implies. It is, however, perhaps justifiable to present the questions that are actually being raised and to show how they are raised. At the risk of presenting something useless, one must venture into "contentious" questions, while remaining aware that what one says has not the same solid foundations as other points.[1]

### Sexual morals: individual or collective morals?

The ethics of relationships and sexual morality does not only concern private questions; it is much broader. Perhaps one of the difficulties with this area of morals is that it concerns both individual and collective questions. Both levels are important, because the morals of relationships and sex cannot be separated from struggles for the collective liberation of people. Our present topic therefore has several dimensions. It includes, among others, the collective liberation of women from oppression by men in our patriarchal society. It concerns our culture, which tends to consider others as

1. The epistemological status of the above requires comment. On the one hand, moralists usually qualify theses as "less well-founded" if they are less in agreement with positions moralists in the past generally accepted. The warning implied by this expression is that certain "readings" may take the public away from the beaten paths of thought and action. However, what are called "well-founded positions" may often raise many questions. People often regret having been imprisoned in old-fashioned ideas. Furthermore, this expression of "less well-founded" also refers to the "rational" coherence of the thesis.

This situation is similar to that which can be found in mathematics; there is always tension between the pure mathematician, who seeks internal consistency in his results, and the applied mathematician, who seeks verified efficiency according to external criteria. So what we might call the "pure philosopher" seeks a thesis with the greatest internal consistency, whereas the "applied philosopher" aims at social change. The criteria for validating a thesis are thus different. In addition, formal coherence often arises after a more intuitive advance. One therefore has to know for whom one is writing and why. I believe that the tension between the two points of view is fertile, both in mathematics and in philosophy. In the latter field, Teilhard de Chardin's struggle with "professional philosophers" can be instructive.

possessions, or as mere parts in a lineage, in that it relates to heritages. Finally, it concerns the story of each individual. In all these aspects, we face sexual ethics as inseparable from other oppressive structures in our society, that is, those that are linked to the production of goods, the political struggle for power, and so forth.

A "sexual liberation," therefore, has economic and political implications; it consequently requires a structural approach. But we are also faced with individuals having to cope with day-to-day decisions in a given society. They do so with their psyche as it has been shaped by our institutions. Their emotional problems may seem trifling compared with a broader social analysis and the society of one's dreams. But it remains true that, for individuals who are always more or less caught up in psycho-social determinisms, the prime question is how to act in a given society. Hence, sexual ethics are first and foremost individual. That is why it is meaningful to state that there is a relative autonomy for the interpersonal aspect compared to the collective one. Even if the solution of individual problems scarcely affects the structural dimension of society, it is of prime importance for every individual. The individual aspect of sexual morality has a status similar to that of psychology. Even if psychological therapeutic methods have no effect on the social conditions underlying neuroses, psychotherapy is nevertheless an essential step for some individuals. Without it, psychological problems can make it impossible to raise more global questions. The same is true of sexual morality. Reducing it to personal questions would truncate it, but avoiding individual questions would divorce it from reality. That is why, just as it is meaningful to recognize the relative autonomy of psychology vis-à-vis sociology, so is it meaningful to recognize the interpersonal aspect of sexual ethics vis-à-vis the collective. What has to be kept in mind, however, is the link between the two aspects and the effect of social change on individuals.

## A changing morality: new interpretations of the language of the body

In our society, sexual ethics are changing. The language of the body, especially sexual and genital languages, no longer have the same significance as they used to. Although some people still stress the importance of the sexual ethic (cf. the Vatican Declaration of January 1976), other people have a different view. Some Christians, for example, scarcely see any contradiction in what they see as a very serious Christian commitment and sexual practices that, only a few years ago, would have been considered libertarian. It is clear that, for many people, sexual ethics is peripheral to ethical themes. While in the past the meaning of sexuality seemed to be obvious, there is now a search for multiple elements of meaning in body language.

### The social standpoint in the new interpretation of body language

Social classes do not all interpret body language in the same way. For much of society, the scope and variety of the language of tenderness is scarcely known. It is not easy, for example, for hard-working blue-collar laborers who are "well-integrated" in our society of production and consumption to think much about sexual behavior. By contrast, one can see an intense search into tenderness and sexuality among the upper middle classes.[2]

2. We should point out that, although the search for new forms of tenderness and their expression is peculiar to the upper middle classes of our society, it is also true that some of the most delicate forms of this behavior are to be found among the underprivileged and even marginal classes. People in such milieux are not concerned with the sexual norms of traditional morals, but often, when not too crushed by the demands of their lives and their social conditions, express enormous tenderness in their relationships.

We may wonder why the upper middle classes are the specific social position where this phenomenon occurs. A first answer would be that the language of the body is less culturally determined for the lower classes. For those who were not "well-born," being without a name, a line, a heritage, there did not seem to be a social need for many strict standards. As long as the behavior of the "people" did not disturb the social order, the people were allowed to get married and make love more or less as they pleased.[3] The same was not true for the upper middle classes and the bourgeoisie. It is therefore not surprising that it was people in those layers of society who were the first to reinterpret the language of the body in an attempt to throw off what they considered a strait jacket.

Furthermore, the privileged classes were, generally speaking, the only ones whose housing accommodations allowed a private life. Without the privacy offered by modern homes, in separate houses or private apartments, it is very difficult to imagine a personal and private choice of sexual behavior. After all, interpreting individual body language is a luxury. In addition, psychologists, training groups, and sensitivity groups are an expense incurred in the search to understand and solve the problems raised by the sexual revolution. For all these reasons, it is fairly understandable that, finally, it was in upper-middle-class circles that the search appeared.

### A revolt of Eros against Logos

When people experience new interpretations of individual body language, they do not think about economic, social,

---

3. Although departures from moral standards were tolerated among the "people," I must stress that dominant ideologies have colonized the whole of society, in particular imposing a patriarchal, phallocratic society everywhere, and reducing women to the status of objects.

and cultural factors. Subjectively, new body language is usually experienced as a revolt of Eros against Logos. This ideology of spontaneity, in fact, tends to conceal the socio-economic elements of the change in emotional and sexual mores.

The German-American philosopher Marcuse has well expressed the meaning of this rediscovery of spontaneity. Freud, whose thought reflects the nineteenth and early twentieth centuries, believed that people should be governed by the reality principle, and that the whole of civilization is based on the limiting of pleasure through reason. Marcuse thought otherwise. Freud, and most Westerners, read the history of civilization as the story of the triumph of reason and its techniques. Marcuse saw the other side of the coin; the history of civilization reveals the function of repression of spontaneity in setting up the particular power structures of our present, economically oriented society. In a double reading of history, Marcuse saw, on the one hand, the conquest of the universe by humanity, and, on the other hand, the repression of pleasure and desire because of the restrictions imposed by realities. According to Freud, we must continue to repress Eros and spontaneity to maintain civilization. In his view, if the principle of pleasure, desire, and the search for satisfaction were to master us, the universe would head for disaster; therefore, the only possibility for the universe to survive is to maintain the work ethic, even if it means repressing spontaneity. Marcuse agreed with the fact that, when our civilization was being built, it was necessary to repress spontaneity and Eros. While Marcuse shared Freud's belief that Western civilization is based on the repression of spontaneity, he added the notion that the reality principle has today been supplanted by the performance principle, which means that people are asked to suppress their spontaneous desires not only to adapt themselves to reality but also to provide the greatest productivity possible. Although an initial repression of spontaneity was necessary to build the world, production has now become an end in itself and that is why (in Marcuse's opinion again) spontaneity is now being over-repressed, that is, repressed in a way not well adapted to present realities. We no longer produce in order to live; rather, we more and more live in order to produce. Our civilization is like that of pioneers who, having started by working hard in order to survive in desert surroundings, continue to strive hard although the infrastructures that they have laid could now enable them to live in a much more relaxed way.

In the beginning, work, and the importance attached to productivity, might have been understandable and justifiable. But later it became over-repression. To Marcuse's mind, the Western world has become one of over-repression, in which everything is dominated by the rationale of production, which has only one aim: obey the technical-social-economic imperatives of production. Under a disguise of rationalism, our society hides the irrationality of productivity sought after as an aim in itself. Western rationality has become a means of internal social control, justified by "scientific positivism" and internalized by individuals who serve as their own wardens in the prisons of their own minds. Thus, the modern form of domination is a cultural one in which people are trapped by their own reason and its perceptions of reality.[4] In the name of reason, administrative bureaucracies present irrational imperatives; and it is against this domination by reason that spontaneity revolts. This

4. This domination is not only cultural; it is also part of the socioeconomic structures, especially in its division of time. On the one hand, time for hard work, on the other, time for leisure, which itself is invaded by the brainwashing of advertising. This concept of separation of time is essential to understanding the background of the reinterpretation of body language.

could be one of the meanings of the sexual revolution. Spontaneity persists, bursting imprisoning discourse that attempts to justify the present morality with reasons that justify nothing.

Thus, the rediscovery of the individual body expresses the revolt of those who believe that they have worked hard enough to build society and who want to start living. Seen in this light, it is not difficult to understand that a revolution of this kind has been made possible by the freedom that characterizes the twentieth-century upper middle classes. Indeed, contrary to the nineteenth-century bourgeoisie, these groups live in a society that is no longer on the edge of famine. They feel they can achieve many things thanks to technology and no longer feel obliged to be permanently defending themselves and "the progress of civilization." However, they have little social power. This explains why they look for new ways of using power where they have some: in their private lives. However, other people experience this bursting of the old codes as a threat. The lower middle classes, that is, those whose social status is relatively uncertain, have to work hard simply to maintain their position and yet still hope to improve it. They thus find themselves very insecure and threatened by the explosion of spontaneity among the upper middle classes. This is understandable when one remembers that the lower middle classes try to identify themselves with the managerial classes, but lack their security. Like all socially rising groups, they are fundamentally conservative. They do not want the world view of the group they are trying to enter to change. Social advancement is not easy, and any changes in the rules might make it impossible. Consequently, such groups prefer to stick to the "solid middle-class values" of work, individual effort, and controlled spontaneity. It is, moreover, in these values that the individual members of these classes place their hopes for eventually achieving a higher social status. We should therefore not be surprised that such people, who feel that they have to work hard to rise in society, fear that too much spontaneity, especially in sexual matters, could be explosive and dangerous. These lower middle classes are therefore generally opposed to the sexual revolution and feel threatened by it. They want to stick to the rules and can easily form a "moral majority."

Conservatives in the upper classes are also opposed to these social changes. They identify with the former social order to which they owe their social status; thus, they oppose changes. They are aware, with a fairly accurate sociological insight, that the revolt of spontaneity is a threat to the established social order. Those who defend the past tend therefore to consider the body and its language with objectivity characteristic of the last century; for them, adultery is adultery and all adultery means the same thing. It is the rule of (apparent) objectivity!

Finally, the upper middle classes also often feel ill at ease with the revolution in body language, which brings out clearly the problem of what interpersonal relationships involve. Since the sexual revolution makes everything possible and imaginable, many types of behavior appear equivalent and thus lose all specific meaning. They all become "the same," and there is no choice that seems to make a difference. The result is emptiness and meaninglessness, the usual outcome of the tendency to make everything connected with sex private and devoid of links to the rest of one's existence.

People involved in the sexual revolution rarely recognize it as a social event; they see it as an individual search. It is thus difficult to analyze it in its social dimension. Two directions seem to be emerging, however. On the one hand, some people, while trying to renovate their body language, are heading for a sort of libertinism. Although such a course of action may be liberating to a certain extent, it often seems to have its limitations. These people seem to search for themselves by exploring their social relationships in training groups, sensitivity groups, psychoanalysis, mate-swapping, and so forth. They seem to want to encounter many people, but it seems that the "otherness" of the "others" is not always recognized. In such circles, the concept of liberation is often limited to an individual dimension, which frequently leads the "liberated" person to feel rootless in society and enclosed in his own "privatized" universe.

On the other hand, the reinterpretation of body language may be a part of a broader liberation, because the social mechanisms of repression of sexuality are seen in relation to other forms of repression and oppression. This process eventually leads to a questioning of broader processes that are as much political as economic and cultural. Then, sexual liberation is linked to other forms of liberation, in particular to those related to production and work relationships. We will come back to this when we discuss structural ethics.

In this world in mutation, feminism appears to be a sphere in which the individual and the collective are joined. Indeed, although the demands of feminists are often linked to individual issues and although their social origin is the middle class (which has the time and the leisure to think about the development of sexuality), they nevertheless do have a social dimension. As soon as the feminist movement starts thinking, it meets collective questions about its participation in a society of dominance, appropriated by males and linked to a whole socioeconomic system.

### Change versus tradition

Change in the sexual ethic is not taking place outside its own historical context. This change has as a background what might be called the traditional view of sexuality. It is impossible to give a clear and precise definition of the traditional picture of sexuality that confronts our period of time.

There is not one single moral code, any more than there is one single traditional society. It nevertheless seems important to explore certain dimensions of the cultural patterns that we have inherited from the past. This version of tradition will obviously be biased and incomplete. It nevertheless seems that from the traces of the past, certain approaches and some global features can be identified. Thus, I assume that it makes sense to talk about "a traditional view" of sexuality that is always present, underlying our present-day ethical reflection.

We will use three approaches to explore this background. First, we will review the evolution of ideas about sexuality from the Middle Ages to the present day, stressing the socioeconomic factors that determined them. Next, we will examine certain ethical positions related to attitudes prevalent in the beginning of this century, those of our grandparents. Finally, to complete this outline of the background of present-day sexual ethics, we will look at the way in which social sciences, especially psychology and sociology, approach sexuality.[5]

5. One has to be careful when using the social sciences to shed light on moral questions. It is particularly important to realize that when one is talking about *the* psychologist, *the* sociologist, etc., it sounds as if there were a universal (and therefore idealistic) determination of their theories. In fact, individual theses are always marked by the socioeconomic position of those who produce them. Moreover, we cannot speak once and for all of *one* psychology of sociology, because at the basis of sciences there are paradigms that are themselves determined by the social standpoint connected with their production. When used in ethics, therefore, these disciplines function outside their own sphere, like outside "experts." This means that they function ideologically, and therefore are likely to be deceptive. It is, however, true to say that, because of these disciplines, questions are raised. Moreover, the disciplines challenge each other. Even if their language is deeply ideological (that is, with ill-defined criteria and hidden contradictions), it exists and functions. To this extent, it is true that anthropology, psychology, and sociology change the way ethics raise questions, but it is not true that they determine ethics.

The history of mores

Although it seems impossible, by means of a straightforward empirical study, to determine one single universal norm for sex, all known societies have general norms concerning it.[6] Every society organizes its emotional and sexual relationships so that the race can survive and the social structures can be consolidated. But these norms are as numerous and diverse as the societies. That is why we will start with our own history: the sexual mores of our Western society.

Interpretations of the past are neither simple nor always coherent. After all, we only inquire about those aspects of the past that interest us, and we always use a more or less subjective frame of reference. Furthermore, attitudes and ethical codes are not always consistent themselves, and even when they are, we do not always see their logic. Nevertheless historians agree that, in the Middle Ages, people were less concerned about questions of sex than our grandparents were. And yet, that was the period when theologians had great difficulty in not finding a kind of sin in any sexual pleasure.

In the Middle Ages, there was a desire for ritual purity concerning sex; after St. Augustine, and under the influence of the Stoics, sexual pleasure was considered impure (it was, for example, forbidden to approach the Eucharist after sexual relations or nocturnal emission). Sexual morality in this period appeared above all to defend lineage and to impose

6. On this point, as on many others, I refer the reader to the work published by a commission of the Catholic Theological Society of America: A. Kosnik et al., *Human Sexuality: New Directions in American Catholic Thought* (Paulist Press, 1977). I refer readers who would like to find a broader context for this chapter to that book. As for norms existing in all cultures, the closest to such a norm would seem to be the prohibition of incest: by this I mean that in all cultures, sexual relations are taboo between two persons having certain familial bonds.

taboos.[7] In modern times, this global approach based on the dialectics of pure and impure gave way to a "rational" view of sexuality, in which the criteria advanced were linked to "reason" or to scientific (or supposedly scientific) arguments. Priority seemed to be given to an ethics concerned with biological heredity and to theories that were more and more concerned with sexuality, until, in the twentieth century, "sexual fulfillment" has, for all practical purposes, become a social norm.

This evolution can be attributed to the profound modifications that took place at the end of the Middle Ages in the Western economic system. Previously, society had been organized on a self-sufficiency basis. The farms, castles, and monasteries were self-sufficient, in that they produced both the products for consumption and a large proportion of the necessary tools. The inhabitants of these units lived in close contact with each other and knew each other in ways that went far beyond the functional necessities that brought them together. There was almost no differentiation of roles in society, and the division of labor was very limited. Relationships were from one individual to another. One did not go to the local cobbler's only to have some shoes made, but also to see old Jack or Robin who made shoes. In this context, people knew each other more as persons than by their social roles, and there was little distinction between rational and emotional life. They were not afraid to touch each other, to drink from the same cup. These differences can, moreover, be seen when one compares human relationships in little villages, which are becoming more and more rare, and those in cities. One could even go so far as to say that in a self-sufficient economy, people still know each other; personal problems, illnesses, emotions, the perception of one's body are

7. Cf. M. Foucault, *The History of Sexuality* (Pantheon, 1978).

not divorced from work and social relationships. In industrial and urban civilizations, by contrast, they are perceived only via their functional relevance. Thus, economic systems and the social relations corresponding to them finally produce cultural conceptions of the body and of sexuality, which in turn mirror the collective system.

The Middle Ages had a different attitude toward property than ours: they did not make of wealth capital to be invested. Production surpluses were not saved in investments to provide for continuous economic growth. In fact, surpluses were usually used up in the aristocracy's sumptuous expenditure, a process that can still be seen in developing countries. This attitude had its consequences in the way people perceived their bodies. Then, time was divided into labor and festivities. The latter were not rational, but burst out in what our economically minded bourgeois minds call "excesses." Capitalists count what they spend on amusement. The peasants of the Middle Ages hardly imposed any limits on themselves when their socioeconomic situation gave them the means. Their sexual ethics was not a calculating ethics.

At the same time, for the aristocrats, the body became a symbol of prestige and expenditure devoted to fighting and feasting (the two being combined in tournaments). This is a long way from the parsimonious nineteenth century, which worried that excesses might be too tiring.

Moralists of the period from the eleventh to the fourteenth centuries often seem to hesitate. They are under the sway of a tradition of ritual purity and the rigor of St. Augustine, who saw original sin in sexuality, and yet some thinkers, like Abelard, Albert the Great, and, to a certain extent, St. Thomas Aquinas, departed from this view to consider sexuality good. They spoke more about virtues to encourage than about faults to discourage, an approach that began to disappear from the time of William of Occam (fourteenth century).

At the end of the Middle Ages, there were great changes. Merchants began to cross Europe in all directions and the relations they had with their customers or with one another were less related to personal feeling than to business and contracts. Slowly the division of labor became more widespread, until it reached the stage we see today. Social roles became more and more varied, to the point that it is now possible for us to deal with someone whom we know only by his job and about whom we know nothing personally. The person is no more a body, but a function. From the economic point of view, surpluses are no longer spent on festivities, but are parsimoniously put away and carefully saved. The bourgeois mind is economical and rational, basing its activities on efficiency and profitability. To achieve this, a calculating self-control has become a fundamental virtue.

In the midst of these socioeconomic changes, the perception of the body changed; it tended more and more to be considered as a means, as a tool, sometimes even (cf. Descartes) as an automaton. The body and social relations lost their affective meaningfulness. Withdrawal, in the psychological sense of the word, took place, and emotions gradually moved into the sphere of private life. This sphere, moreover, set up its own barriers and protective system. This was when it became immodest to be naked and when bodies had to be kept clean; bedrooms became different from living rooms. Like all other possessions, bodies became more and more the objects of calculations, which medicine, and later psychology, determinedly managed. In large cities, neighbors more and more came to be strangers. We have reached the stage today where, when someone greets us, we wonder what he is after. Feelings having fled into people's interior life, where they are expressed in romantic outbursts, the rest of social life is today based on calculations and business. Books on morals, for their part, seem to be more and more concerned with the body, with trying to control it and turn it into a calm, sober, well-ordered tool, ready to work or to procreate. For this to happen, internalized proscriptions have multiplied.

What was repressed in daily life began to produce undercurrents, which manifested themselves in many different ways. For example, although it was proclaimed that "one does not talk about such things," many pedagogical, moral, and medical essays were written about sexuality. The body was carefully covered up, but the smallest area of exposed skin seemed to be full of an erotic power, in a way that the wise maid in Molière's *Tartuffe* mocked. A sort of hide-and-seek was played around sexuality. This game has probably reached its climax in today's beach phenomenon: the game of sex is exhibited, mastered, and challenged in a leisure institution. Freud brought these multiple changes to light. The theory of psychoanalysis can be seen as our society's attempt to handle and manage the problems raised by this disassociation of the body and human relations.

It is against this historical background that we should regard the patterns of sexual ethics that influence today's discussions of sexuality.

### The sexual ethics of our grandparents

The most striking aspect of a "traditional"[8] textbook on morals is the importance it attaches to the physical side. It obviously deals with the body and bodily actions. And yet even a superficial glance shows that, behind the physical aspect of the body, social relations are present. To understand the importance attached to the body, we must first remember

8. That is, one having the imprint of both the agrarian tradition and puritan ethics.

that it is through sex that the human race reproduces itself. This reproduction, with all its socioeconomic implications, is central to any understanding of sexual morality. Furthermore, we should remember that, in the agrarian society— and even in the early industrial period—the number of one's children was a guarantee of wealth and a secure old age. Sexuality, the basis of this wealth, was considered a blessing. Because of this, relations with a woman were often marked by a tendency to consider first of all how fertile she was, how good a producer of wealth.

Sexual behavior plays an important role in the organization of society. Anthropologists have pointed out that the exchange of women is often one of the essential elements in economic and political transactions. These matrimonial alliances knit a social network and reinforce economic and political links. Thus, the daughter of a landowner brings as dowry to the heir of the neighboring estate a long-desired field; or the marriage of a prince consolidates a treaty. To protect these bonds, explicit or implicit norms protect against misalliances. These norms really concern the dominant classes more than the ordinary people. Included amongst their functions is that of protecting and socially controlling the privileged classes. Sexual ethics thus help to identify and consolidate the dominant social groups. The example of the aristocracy is typical in this respect. It speaks in a very significant way of "well-born" people. Another example of the relationship between sexual norms and social organization is that our society is patriarchal, or based on the male line: this is reflected in the laws, which, until quite recently, universally sanctioned inequalities between the sexes.

Sexual ethics therefore works to guarantee the maintenance of the established order, and often the privileges that are related to it, as well. How often do we hear people say, "If that's allowed now, what will be next!" Sometimes societies allow certain departures from the code, as long as they do not endanger the social order. For example, until recently bastards were acceptable on the condition that they be able to come into an inheritance.

Thus, contrary to the more or less individualistic way in which it is usually presented, sexual morality does refer to social structures. But there is more to it than that: we must not underestimate the concern for persons in traditional sexual morals. We can note, for example, that since the Middle Ages women have attained more acceptable places in society. The Church's effort, for example, to maintain a stable sexual ethic can be seen as an attempt to prevent men from completely dominating women and making women purely and simply tools for reproduction, or economic and political items of exchange.

The traditional sexual ethic has a normative aspect. Sexual behavior is limited according to age, partner, and acts. First, it is not acceptable for the very young; nor, in a more subtle way, for the old (which could be related to a trend to limit sexual behavior to reproduction).[9] A second limitation concerns the partner. Traditional ethics textbooks forbade autoeroticism, incest, and homosexuality; they assumed monogamy within the institution of marriage, which was closely linked to the social and economic order. Third, traditional sexual morals define forms of sexual behavior, which are divided into the acceptable and the forbidden. A typical example of forbidden behavior is the traditional prohibition of contraception. Finally, sexual ethics provide a way of viewing the responsibility of people: one should aim at the development of the spouse, the children, and society. But, at the same time, this traditional approach sanctions a certain number of inequalities in roles, especially in the secondary role attributed to women.

9. In the distant past of Christianity, the acceptability of sexual relations in cases of sterility was much discussed. It is remarkable to see how, until quite recently, the sexuality of older people was considered with an ironic smile.

Traditional ethics are summed up well in all the norms concerning the institution of marriage and the family. In the traditional system, the stability of the family system is considered most important, together with everything that it represents at the social, economic, and political levels. It is not for nothing that, at the end of the nineteenth century, the family was considered a pillar of society. It was the institution that kept everybody in their "place."

Indeed, as long as anybody was "somebody," there was only a limited choice of partner. We could say that marriage was considered too serious for an explosive feeling like love to have any real place in it. A wedding was more of a political-economic contract, in which the families came together in an alliance. It is significant that sexual morality was not considered an interpersonal question, but rather a question concerning social organization as a whole. Only recently has sexuality been "privatized" to the extent of no longer being the subject of social norms. This movement, which started during the Renaissance, has reached its culmination in the Scandinavian societies, where the legal forms of marriage are more and more taking the shape of private contracts.

As far as waiting until after marriage before having intercourse is concerned, our "grandparents' ethics" seem to have stressed two important factors. First, intercourse could lead to pregnancy, and a family was expected to be prepared before a child appeared, to have a social unit ready to receive it. Second, waiting for marriage before having intercourse humanized sexuality; this wait, like any delay in satisfying a desire, made it possible to invest other feelings than just the immediate satisfaction of a desire. Furthermore, waiting for marriage before having sexual relations could be interpreted as a subtle way of defending women's rights. If sexual relations took place before the wedding, the woman was in danger of becoming a mother in a society that was not yet ready to welcome her child. Seen in this way, waiting for marriage before having sexual relations can be considered as a right for women that protected them from the arbitrary whims of men.

The importance given to the public commitment involved in a wedding can also be understood in this light. For a long time, in the Middle Ages, weddings were allowed to take place semi-privately, without any witnesses. According to some historians, the Church's insistence that weddings be public had a liberating effect on women, who could no longer be abandoned with their children if the men did not want them. In addition, publicly making promises introduces an important psychological element: anything public no longer belongs solely to the couple's imagination, so it can no longer be "read" arbitrarily by either of them. Even today, many people hesitate to make the formal bonds that bind them to someone whom they consider more or less as a spouse. In a certain number of cases, there is a fear of having an "objective" social relationship and of the loss of some subjective feeling, linked to the public nature of an oath.

I should also point out the importance attached to fidelity within the institution of marriage. This fidelity, in my opinion, is ambiguous. It first means faithfulness to the line of inheritance, to the economic and social order; but it also means that faithfulness that provides the spouse and the children psychological assurance and a certain basic security. Unfortunately, fidelity has almost solely been related to sexual behavior, perhaps to the detriment of a more global faithfulness to the members of the family.

Finally, the institution of marriage is, in traditional society, at the heart of social life: it controls the inheritance of titles and goods, it introduces alliances and gives everybody a status. Social security is also insured through the family. In today's world, however, marriage and the family are becoming a more and more peripheral institution, as both lose their influence over social life and become more and more centered on themselves. At the same time, sexual morality is becoming more and more "privatized." [10]

## The religious background of
## traditional morals

Traditionally in the West, as in most cultures, sexual morals have been related to religion. Thus, physical acts have been sacralized to the extent of sometimes even giving them a sort of immediate meaning. Thus, in the Middle Ages, we saw that someone who had had "nighttime pollution" was refused the Eucharist, and modern books on moral theology defined sins through physical descriptions of sexual acts.

But, in counterpoint to this "sacralization" of behavior, religion also promotes the value of the relationship between the spouses. Human love is accorded great value through the inspiration of the biblical theme of the alliance of God with his people. Through this theme, which has been fairly central to Christian marriage ever since St. Paul, human love has been "read" in the same categories as the love of God for his people. Just as God was first to love and free his people, so spouses were called to love and liberate one another. Fidelity then goes beyond obedience to a socioeconomic contract, to feed itself on the theme of God's loving his people even when they are unfaithful to God. Faithfulness becomes a perspective in which, despite all human vicissitudes and sins, despite limitations and friction, an alliance is built up and an encounter takes place.

In the same way, the whole Christian tradition stresses that no person can be considered the possession of another. Although in many respects this tradition had continued to

10. It is privatized even if sexual life is also commercialized, like everything private in our society. Commercialization is another social controlling device.

assume inequality between men and women, there is in it an expression of equality between human beings, who are recognized as persons first, and men and women second. The notions of forgiveness, of selfless acceptance of the other, of liberation from physical, economic, and social oppression become, in this view, central to relationships. In this same vision of a God who loves his people so much that he gave his life for them, Christian marriage is perceived as the possibility of "giving oneself to another." It becomes possible for the partner to say with trust or with faith: "Here is my life for you." This obviously relates to the Christian theme of the Eucharist, which reminds people how Jesus said: "Here is my body," that is, "my life."

It may be useful here to add a few words about the Catholic Church's position on sexual ethics. This is a difficult task, because, first, the church is not simply the hierarchy, and, second, history has shown unexpected developments in the hierarchy's positions. When the Catholic Church approaches questions of doctrine and morals, it recognizes the important role of the so-called Magisterium, that is, the Pope and the bishops, assisted by the theologians and the discernment of the people of God under the guidance of the Spirit. Concerning sexual ethics, "Rome" has adopted several positions. For example, in 1968, the encyclical "Humanae Vitae" stated that contraception by non-natural methods was not morally acceptable. A recent paper from the Congregation of the Doctrine of Faith stated that masturbation, homosexuality, and premarital relations were objectively (but not necessarily subjectively) sinful. Its position can thus be qualified as "conservative."

Catholics still face an important question: how to relate to official guidance and see in what way it can help the people of God find their way under the guidance of the Spirit.[11]

11. It is important to see these documents in the light of Church history and traditions and not conclude that the Church's approach to these questions is

The following points, among others, obviously merit re-flection. Is it not true that the Church invites people to per-ceive, in a society that sometimes forgets, that: (a) In emo-tional relationships and in sexuality, the meaning of one's existence is also at stake. (b) The sincerity of one's behav-ior is not everything: consequences go beyond intentions. (c) The body is also the place of the gift of God, the temple of

---

fixed. Furthermore, it is probably wise to note that many moralists have stressed the weakness of some of the philosophical and theological argu-ments raised in these papers, which nobody has ever claimed to be "infalli-ble." The Church must not get trapped too quickly in a corner, preventing further developments. The reader who would like to explore more deeply the ways in which theologians try to throw light on these complex questions will do well to consult Kosnick et al., *Human Sexuality*, or also, Philip S. Keane, *Sexual Morality: A Catholic Perspective* (Paulist Press, 1977).

Perhaps it would be useful to describe Catholic theology's usual atti-tude toward the Magisterium's documents. Catholics are expected to respect the documents' proposals and to follow their guidelines. If, however, in their conscience, they feel they can act differently, they must also respect their conscience. Positions contrary to the Magisterium's must be taken with care, if the expression of disagreement of Catholics is to be legitimate. In their pastoral work, those who have responsibilities must enlighten Chris-tians on the hierarchical authority's positions by presenting them as such, as the continuation of a tradition at the moment when they are published; this implies making balanced comments about the non-absolute nature of the documents, the degrees of importance to be attached to each, and the pos-sibilities of evolution in their interpretation. All Christians, but theologians in particular, are asked also to take part in the Church-wide work to refine the Church's positions where necessary, to define them more precisely, and to correct them. For example, it is after this type of reflection that today prac-tically everybody considers the documents claiming that Moses wrote the Pentateuch as out of date. Church doctrine can develop and change.

Although the historical nature of the authority's directives should be borne in mind, the continuity of the Church's teachings should not be ne-glected. The great majority of theologians agrees that moral principles that have been held by the Church for centuries and that are presented today as ecclesiastical doctrine by all the bishops should be recognized as part of the moral teaching of the Church. On the role of the Magisterium in the Catholic Church, see Mgr. A. Deschamps, "Théologie et Magistère," *Ephemerides Theologicae Lovanienses* 72 (1976): 82–133; and R. McCornick, S.J., "Con-science, Theologians and the Magisterium," *New Catholic World* 220, no. 1320 (1977): 268–72.

God, and we are all members of the body of Christ. (d) As St. Paul says, "I am free to do anything. Yes; but not everything is for my good" (I Cor. 6 : 12). (e) If Christ frees us, it is not so that we shall become the slaves of our passions.

This is probably what ecclesiastical documents tend to make concrete with certain (sometimes more or less relevant) statements concerning sexual behavior.

### The ideologies associated with psychology

In connection with a number of themes traditional to the Western and Christian world, modern psychological theories have introduced new ways of looking at sexuality. At least in its popularized form, a certain type of modern psychology has contributed the theme of *growth*. In it, human life is seen as a way of growing, as a kind of search. In this search, like those who sought the Holy Grail, human beings go from one stage to another, from development to development, looking for something they miss, without this "lack" always being clearly defined. Thus, in many different ways, psychologists, such as Erikson, have described stages in the growth of people. They speak of the passages from autoeroticism to hetero-erotocism, from isolation to communication, from fear to trust, from intimacy enclosed upon oneself to responsibility open onto society, and finally from responsibility to a wisdom that more or less manages to live with what is missing, in other words, that deals with death.

However, these themes, although they have an obvious strength and lend meaning to many things, also have some ambiguities. As far as sexuality and relationships are concerned, the theme of growth offers a representation of life built on growth, on fulfillment, on expectations for the future, and on liberation. In this way, popular psychology frees people from a morality that imposes on them certain models, without each individual's path being reverenced in all its diverse meanings. It helps to build human "stories" in which human beings are heading somewhere, even though they travel along lines that are sometimes straight, sometimes curved, sometimes broken. The theme of growth also liberates people from a kind of objective attitude in morals that considers each individual's path as secondary. Obviously, psychology has opened new possibilities for many.

However, this ideology of growth and liberation can be a mask for profound oppression. By always encouraging the search for another place, for a future, it may prevent people from living their existence simply. By freeing people from some commandments and prohibitions, it may impose another norm that is just as oppressive: that of perpetual striving. The "perfectly fulfilled couple" can be a very discouraging model. Finally, by presenting the model of the person who is continually progressing and growing, it may cause guilt in those who suffer from the limits of their psychology and of their social situation. From all these points of view, the social standpoint of these approaches in psychology appears to be that of people for whom *something else* appears possible. It is the social situation of more or less privileged people. This ideology of growth is also part of one of industrial society's controlling devices. People have to grow and make progress, and that co-opts them into the system.

Finally, psychology often leads to the popular presentation of a normative image of the ideal human being under the cover of a scientific theory. A critical view of psychological sciences, however, shows that their sources lie in a fairly individual ideological vision that does not always take the social context into account. One may appreciate their contribution to the understanding of sexual behavior, but one must also recognize this limit to that contribution.

Sexual ethics and social sciences

In our society, most of what is said about sexuality is expressed in terms of psychology, but sociological research is used more and more. Whereas psychology usually tries to bring behavior to the level of individual motivations and decisions, sociology tends to link it to social structures and functions. Hence, sociologists point out that, in our society, emotional and sexual relationships are often experienced as private property is. The members of a couple "belong" to each other. Each possesses and is possessed. Each has rights over the body of the other. Each also has rights over the fruit of the union: the children. According to this "reading," emotional relationships are mainly perceived in terms of social and economic paradigms. Marriage is an exchange, perhaps even an exchange of goods. Indeed, in some cases, it seems as if a man is buying his wife. The "dowry" of some cultures seems to suggest that the wife buys a husband, or rather, that the family buys a husband for the daughter.

Modern sociology pays great attention to the structure of the family itself. It points out that heterosexual relationships in our society cannot be understood without examining the family socioeconomic system. Hence, inasmuch as the man earns the money and possessions, the woman can play only a submissive role. That is, indeed, one of the points that feminists are most sensitive about. If women are not paid for the services demanded of them, they automatically become "kept women." In that situation, they are kept in a state of inferiority. Sociological analysis thus shows us that, at least in our society, heterosexual relationships are fundamentally ones of inequality and domination. This remark may, moreover, open the way to some quite new and interesting perspectives in sexual ethics. Ethical and "good" behavior would be any behavior that tends to break down the male domination of women that is introduced by the way our culture perceives sexuality. In other words, behavior and habits would be considered ethical if they led spouses to stop considering themselves as the property of each other. We shall see below how far such perspectives are from ethics based on the defence of lineage and its order.

Social sciences shed some light on the relations between sexual behavior and collective structures, but they do so differently according to the social solidarity and standpoint of sociologists. Sociological studies linked to the feminist movement are particularly sensitive to the man/woman oppression. Marxist-based analyses stress the relationship between the family system and the dominant economic order. They show, for example, the links in Western Europe between the defense of patriarchal lineage and the sexual code, or between the work ethic of bourgeois capitalism and the ethics of the body. Neither of these analyses is neutral: each reflects a point of view.

### Towards a new sexual ethic

Beyond the biological point of view

In traditional textbooks on morals, chastity (that is, the virtue of appropriate sexual behavior) has often been presented from a point of view that stresses the biological and physical aspects of relations. Many moralists seemed to consider that chastity was a virtue concerning sexual pleasure. Such a view attaches great importance to the body, feelings, and genital aspects, each taken separately. It gives less consideration to human relations taken globally, incorporating the body, feelings, genital aspects, and so forth in a more broadly significant context. Seen in this way, moral criteria sometimes seem to be limited to the physical level. The question often raised is: Is such and such sexual pleasure acceptable or not? A rare question is: What do these relations, seen in all their dimensions, do for the people concerned? From the physical or biological point of view, the moralist asks: Are sexual relations or an exchange of tenderness of such and such a type acceptable? But these experiences are usually considered for themselves alone, partially withdrawn from the context of relationships, which gives them their meaning. The language of the body is considered objective and unambiguous.

This point of view is easy to understand when one remembers that, in the past, sexual relations necessarily implied the possibility (or the danger) of pregnancy. This possibility weighed so heavily in the balance that interpersonal relations were considered relatively unimportant. That kind of sexual morality could perhaps be called the defense of the body in its physical dimension. The significance of such a defense can easily be understood when one realizes that the protected body was the body that could produce babies at a time when neither the parents nor society could provide for them. Seen in this way, the physical or biological approach to sexual ethics is not without meaning. Indeed, if the body were not defended, society, and consequently individuals, could suffer great damage. Since emotional drives are very strong, it is understandable that the best defense was to avoid dangerous emotional commitments and erect barriers against them. Hence the tendency to reduce the ethics of emotional relationships to norms concerning physical behavior.

However, that approach has a serious disadvantage: it separates the body from human relations taken in their entirety. This is certainly what happens when a single interpretation is given to particular sexual behavior without realizing that, depending on the context, that same behavior could have different meanings. Consequences of these behaviors show this difference clearly; people have occasionally been psychologically demolished by a smile, while there have been situations in which extramarital physical in-

timacy did not hurt the individuals involved. We may therefore wonder whether it makes sense to attribute a meaning to
a physical sexual act as such.[12] Should it not always be related to its meaning in a relationship? Would it not make
sense to abandon the term sexual morals, which is too
closely associated with the physical aspect of sex, and replace it with the more general one of "morals of emotional
relationships"—which, after all, always have a physical
dimension?

Belittling the intrinsic importance of some physical or
biological aspects of behavior does not mean that they can be
taken lightly, or that their meaning is absolutely arbitrary. On
the contrary, it would seem that sexual behavior, like other
behavior, has meanings that individuals cannot modify as
they like. These meanings may come either from the culture
(which no one individual masters), or from biological evolution. Physical intimacy thus has meanings that individuals
cannot modify at will.

The meaning of physical behavior is not fixed once and
for all, however. One only has to consider cultural differences to prove this. For example, kissing somebody may

12. The expression "sexual act" is used here, as in most books on ethics, in a
way similar to that used by behaviorist psychologists. This use separates
from the act the emotional involvement, thus leading to the deadlock already pointed out. Other approaches consider sexuality as a global human
language.

The following passage from J.-P. Jossua, *L'écoute et l'attente* (Paris:
Cerf, 1978), p. 83, may be helpful. Regarding the meaning of sexual relations, in "a truer, simpler place, we would see that there is no reason for
making such a fuss about them (either to exalt them or to condemn them),
and we could admit that for many people (clerical or lay, single or married)
it is not the most important factor, at least not in every relationship and at all
ages. 'Success' in sexual life is measured according to desire, not to any
rules about virility or femininity. Perhaps those who call themselves
'chaste,' or are satisfied as they say, to lead a life 'sexuated' but not 'sexual'
(without realizing how many equivalents to the sex act they experience if
only through words) are simply those who do not grasp the metamorphoses
of their desire."

have far more meaning in some cultures than in others. What is considered a very moderate sign of affection in some cultures may, elsewhere, signify a much deeper involvement. Consequently, one can say fairly accurately that the signs of tenderness constitute a language that can be used in many ways to express many things, according to the individuals' culture, feelings, situation, and responsibilities. What this kind of language implies, however, is very important to human beings, and therefore should not be treated lightly. Physical involvement plays an extremely important part in human relations, but it is not the sole determinant of the meaning of behavior.

There are many other things to be considered in an act, including everything that is desired or wished for, consciously or unconsciously. Actually, the unconscious structures that guide some behavior should be considered with greater attention, especially in education. Much damage is caused by people who let their unconscious desires overwhelm and deceive them. Unfortunately, those who brought up and taught these people never said anything about the subconscious structures of a psyche. Furthermore, it is important to stress that the consequences of our acts are there, whatever our conscious or unconscious intentions. To that extent, there is an obvious objectivity in sexual ethics.

Thus, a particular type of traditional morals, which examines sexual behavior from the biological or physical point of view without situating it in a broader context of meaning, seems to lead to a deadlock. That kind of description is obviously inadequate. One can nevertheless recognize some meaning to such a description, for two reasons. First, in our culture, moral questions are often raised in these terms, and consequently it makes sense to listen to such a point of view, even if only to show that it is insufficient. Second, physical actions carry with them—at least in our culture, and perhaps for all human beings—meanings that we do not entirely control that have to be taken into account. The major mistake of the physical interpretation would seem to be the (epistemological) decision to separate in the description of human activity the "physical" dimension from its emotional content. This kind of separation is always of doubtful value, because human beings *are* their bodies, they don't just *use* them. Sexual activities do not *have* a meaning, they *are* language, and therefore, in each particular context, are filled with meaning.

From the point of view of ethics, the biological or physical approach almost automatically leads to what we might call a morality of taboos. Some types of sexual behavior, even when separated from the contexts that give them their meaning, are considered acceptable, others are taboo. This explains why a large number of moralists have abandoned this type of "objective" criteria, to say that the ultimate criterion of morals is love.

### The idealistic point of view: love

The point of view that we examine here is based on the premise that there is such a thing as "true love." It presupposes that behavior that expresses this true love is good, and behavior that does not express it is bad. Thus, the criteria deal, not with descriptions of physical behavior, but with the idea of love itself. Physical intimacy is not considered to necessarily have direct significance in itself; rather, the question becomes: Does such and such behavior in a given context express true love, or not? On the basis of this idea of love, some kind of reflection can be worked out for sexual ethics to understand the meanings expressed in behavior and compare them with true love. For example, masturbation might be considered immoral in some well-defined situations in which it might prevent interpersonal love from growing. The interesting aspect is that in this approach, masturbation is not considered non-valid in itself. Only the total meaning that it may have in a given context can make it non-valid.[13] This point of view can be linked to what English-speaking people often call "situational ethics": the situation determines the meaning of an action.[14]

At first sight, the criterion of love works very well and can be very liberating. People no longer feel they are catalogued and labeled, as they are in the physical approach. Moreover, this idealistic point of view happily leaves a place for ambiguous growth, that is, growth that has a meaning that has not yet been grasped. In the ambiguous situations, one can value a behavior that may lead to true love even though, for some reason or other, it cannot yet entirely express love. Furthermore, this point of view gives much more importance to intentions than objective biological morals do. In it, behavior is not abstracted from the basic direction of the interpersonal life of individuals; rather, the basic direction an individual takes is considered to show how that person grows or does not grow toward a true and ideal love. This approach of emotional relations has opened up new horizons for many people who formerly felt trapped in a proscriptive ethic.

Nevertheless, closer examination reveals that this idealistic point of view has several limitations. After all, one may well wonder if there is such a thing as a well-defined concept of true love. And even if such a concept exists, who can say what it is? This raises a fundamental question: does

13. Some people believe that the very act of masturbation carries with it an intrinsic meaning contrary to love. In that case, its meaning is not related to a context, but comes from the very "nature" of the act.

14. This is a different point of view from that of some French existentialists, who say meaning is freely created, no objectivity being possible.

the idealistic point of view give any operational criteria by which to evaluate behavior? The answer seems to be negative, because it does not say at all how to identify true love. Indeed, experience shows that people have very different ideas about that concept, according to their experiences, their culture, and their socioeconomic situation. Some might say that a situation expresses true love, while others would say the opposite. Because the concept of true love is not operational unless it is clearly defined, such disciplines as philosophy, anthropology, psychology, and sociology have been asked to define love. But because they can only define something according to their paradigms, they can only define true love by tinting culturally accepted prejudices with their own outlook. Moreover, anthropology and the theory of ideologies show that there is virtually no universal base for all the statements about what love might be, and it is usually possible to show the relationship between "scientific" conceptions of love and the dominant ideologies of the cultures that produced them. For example, the concept of love, or of normality, promoted by American psychologists often reflects quite closely American culture and mythology. The "cost/benefit" analysis through which behaviorists analyze human decisions is not unrelated to the American way of aiming at profit in all things. The same is true of those who define "true" love as a form of "creative growth."[15]

We are led to recognize that, because it is impossible for everyone to agree on what love is, it is not practical to say that good sexual behavior must be an expression of true love. Thus the whole idealistic point of view is called into question. That people have conflicting ideas about love is fairly obvious, both among couples trying to share how they want to love and among groups that lobby to promote their own

15. Cf. Kosnik et al., *Human Sexuality*.

ideas about love. For example, ask a gay person if homosexual love can be true love, and the response will be yes,
whereas others will call such love unnatural. That is why I
believe that the idealistic concept of love, when presented as
universal and normative, is an empty concept. The same is
true, moreover, of other criteria that ignore the background of
conflict that general concepts conceal.[16]

The concept of love, therefore, seems to be a general one,
under which we collect a variety of behaviors, some very different from each other. Every time someone talks about true
love, remember that it is the point of view of specific people
or groups, using their own particular criteria, and that these
relative criteria cause people to say that certain types of relations are not really "love," while others are. In the same way,
the idea that love is a state one can achieve is completely
misleading. Giving up such ideas is sometimes difficult for
people whose culture has accustomed them to speaking of
love as something to be contrasted with egoism. No doubt
one of the greatest contributions of psychoanalysis is to have
shown that tenderness, hate, aggressiveness, jealousy, desire,
creativity, regression, detachment and involvement, gener-
osity and selfishness, could intermingle. It is impossible to
say that some of these feelings must be present or absent in
"love," or be more or less there. All behavior is a synthesis of
very different desires and feelings. Ethics tries to describe
what types of behavior we want and what types we do not
want. In so doing, however, it is important to be aware that
our choices are always based on particular cultures, social
positions, and myths. Consequently, the moralist who sug-
gests certain types of behavior cannot speak from "nowhere,"
but must suggest one possible way out of many; and it is in
this context that we can speak of a "calling ethics."

16. For example, "the creative growth which aims at integration," mentioned
in Kosnik et al., *Human Sexuality*, as criteria of valid sexuality; such a concept is based on the individual taken in isolation.

Sexuality and liberation

Once we perceive the ambiguities of a universal concept of love,[17] it scarcely makes sense to offer norms as if they were born of such a concept; and once we abandon "universal" language, we must confront many people describing and offering behavior and attitudes that they value from their and their group's point of view. To put it another way, a moralist is an agent for social change: what is at stake is what the moralist wants to change in given sexual situations.

I believe that what leads people to experience a liberation constitutes a valid criterion for emotional relations. That kind of approach has a significant advantage over normative concepts of love because it accepts from the outset the ambiguity and conflictive nature of emotional relationships. Liberation is described, not in terms of a general concept of liberty, but in terms of concretely analyzable situations that the moralist perceives as alienating or oppressing.

The basic ambiguity in emotional relationships is worthy of more detailed examination. It is a matter not simply of recognizing that an emotional relationship can cause blossoming or destruction, but of seeing how the roots of our emotions go deep into the social universe, which affects our emotional life in all its dimensions. Our man/woman relationships are situated in a patriarchal society in which the man is the possessor and the master. Women are so negligible that Freud was able to set up an essentially masculine psychoanalytical model. Economically, in the middle class, until very recently, only men were supposed to earn a living, while women were almost automatically servants at home. Women were considered their husband's possession, and they themselves tried to "keep" him. To defend this "property," a whole moral code was worked out that mixed ethical

17. Cf. Chapters 2 and 3 on this subject.

imperatives with legal restraints. Sexual morals are often a way of protecting a certain way of life related to the oppression of women by men; this can only be understood if one thinks also about the role of the family structure in the defense of economic heritages. Furthermore, certain expressions, such as "*my* wife," "*my* husband," are not simply polite formulas, but often show that relations within the couple are not unlike the private ownership by one person of another. As for men, they are prisoners of their privileges and of that male pride that society inculcates into them. Our culture expects men to behave like masters and to hide their feelings, and that is a very alienating situation. The same culture imposes on women the passive behavior of a dependent subject. In addition, encounters between the sexes take on the style of competition and conquest, and so resemble the competition prevalent in our economic system. Finally, in the cultural, sexual, and genital ritual, a certain amount of aggression, domination, and wile is found, in which the partners consider each other as prey. To a certain extent, man/woman relations seem to display all the characteristics of social domination. Yet they also express human hopes to the greatest extent when they are lived with tenderness, forgiveness, and reconciliation.

These cultural models are not isolated elements in our culture. Nor do they reflect the malice of particular individuals. They form part of an economic, political, and cultural system in which mutual oppression is the rule. We cannot, therefore, isolate questions of emotions from the global societal system. The fundamental ambiguities in our relationships are only one aspect of something much more global that religious tradition has called "original sin," that Marxist philosophy reads in terms of the class struggle, and that psychoanalysis links to the first experiences of the child in its family. Each speaks of a basic ambiguity or a fundamental disorder. We are all united in and, to a certain extent, accomplices in this ambiguity, but we are not responsible for it personally. It is the recognition of this fundamental disorder from which we want to get away that gives meaning to the word "liberation."

Seen in this way, the word "chastity," which in the moralists' language means, not sexual abstinence, but a way of living "well" with respect to sexuality, could be defined in connection with emotional relationships in the following way: interpersonal relations that liberate from individual and social domination, whether of an external nature or internalized, are chaste. Chastity is a way of living one's relationships so that they do not lead to domination, or at least lead to as little domination as possible. Against this utopian background, we could dream of a society in which sex drives would not be used for mutual exploitation, in which the language of the body would not be overinfluenced by the fear of domination by the other, in which individuals would not be crushed by over-internalized proscriptions, and in which the body could simultaneously express the gratuitousness and the creative aspect of any human encounter.

As a first approach, we can say that some ways of loving—for example, those that enable a man to live his feelings without imprisoning him in the stereotyped image of the self-assured and unfeeling being—will free those who love each other in the midst of ambiguities. Other types of relationships, however—such as those that lead a woman to behave as a subordinate—will make lovers even more the prisoners of their social position. Some kinds of relationships thrust people into the universe of domination, where things and bodies are for possession and domination. However, others appear on the utopian but significant background of a universe in which human beings recognize and accept each other. In that universe, things and bodies are expressions of people. This contrast gives meaning to the word "chastity." These criteria do not offer an ideal to achieve, but a liberation process to be recognized.[18] In a given situation, some types of behavior are considered as definitely liberating, others as less so. For example, it is possible that a homosexual phase might be very liberating and represent a step towards a deeper liberation if, for example, it enables someone to be less afraid of his or her body and feelings.[19]

Of course, that kind of liberation may not be only a way of feeling at ease personally. Just as the fundamental disorder I mentioned above touches all the dimensions of human life, so it is simplistic to think of chastity solely in psychological terms. Although the interpersonal and individual levels have their own autonomy—it is always I who live my life and I am my body—we have to see how our emotional and interpersonal relationships are linked to society's political, economic, and cultural structures. The utopian background against which I hope to present sexual ethics is, therefore, the vision of a world without domination, that is, a world in which no one is absolutely dependent on another to live his or her own existence. This applies at the individual and collective levels.

By speaking of relations of dominance concerning sexuality in our Western culture today, I do not mean to refer to an abstract and general concept of oppression, but more particularly to that particular aspect of our culture known as "sexism." This refers to the ideologies that base relations of domination on differences of sex. I do not believe, therefore, that it is possible to speak of chastity in general; it is important to start from a particular point of view in our civilization

18. The point of view I am putting forward refuses to offer a *general* ideal, given once and for all, but wants to promote *local* ethical reflection: in a given situation, analyzed by those involved as oppressing and alienating, local reflection tries to see how some liberation can occur.

19. It is obvious that, by this statement, I am speaking of concrete experience, not presenting homosexuality as an abstract ideal.

in which, historically, women are not considered persons and men are considered masters.[20] Women are oppressed, while men are alienated. We live in a culture in which people are not considered equals; the masculine stereotype sees women from a specific point of view, determined by men, that is, from the point of view of the master, the possessor. In this way, any man/woman relationship can either accentuate this domination, or liberate itself from it. This might provide us with concrete criteria to understand what chastity might be between a man and a woman. Chastity in behavior could be measured by how it enables the man and the woman to get out of their stereotypes, whereas behavior that reinforces those stereotypes would be the opposite of chastity. For example, behavior by which the man made the woman his property or vice-versa would according to this criterion be unchaste. The same kind of analysis could be carried out on the basis of all types of behavior and feelings present in tenderness and physical love. Some types reinforce the domination and oppression present in our culture, while others free people from them.

Presented in this way, ethics related to chastity are no longer situated in a timeless universe, but are seen in a concrete way to be related to what men and women are in a particular culture and particular situations. Thus, the liberation of women would be found in the possibilities they obtain of asserting themselves, and chastity would go so far as to ask

20. To understand this link between masculinity and domination versus femininity and submission, a little exercise can be helpful. Write on a piece of paper all the psychological traits, qualities, and defects usually attributed to a group of "masters"; next, write the qualities, defects, and psychological features of a dominated group. Later, as another exercise, do the same for masculine and feminine psychological features. It will be easy to see that the so-called male qualities almost coincide with the qualities of the dominant groups, while the female features will coincide with those of the dominated groups.

questions about the division of the household income and the type of relations that that may create. Similarly, it would be impossible to think of chastity without questioning the division of labor between men and women. In a society that in order to survive had to devote all its energies to increasing its population, women had to concentrate on their role as mothers. This is the origin of the division of labor between the sexes. Women looked after maintenance and logistics, while men got on with outside tasks and external objectives. This division of labor is at the root of our society's oppression of women; their liberation will therefore demand a modification in so-called "masculine" and "feminine" roles. In the meantime, new ways of relating will little by little free men from everything they have to do to maintain their position as masters, and women from having to behave submissively.

At first sight, such criteria may seem strange and far removed from the usual experience of love. They do, however, have the advantage of relating sexuality to other aspects of behavior in relationships. It is, indeed, commonly recognized that love should liberate a person from the fear of being used by the other, and enable body language to be simply the expression of a mutual recognition as persons or of the wish to procreate together, whereas "unchaste" love is possession, manipulation. It is obviously not merely because a person has some sexual pleasure with another that their behavior can be described as positive or negative from an ethical point of view. It is only from the relationship that sexual pleasure will take its meaning.

### Marriage and family

There is, in the point of view developed above, a relationship between chastity and the economic organization of the family, just as there is with the temptation for men to control and hold power in a patriarchal society. Also, we cannot neglect the way in which, in our society, marriage has become a way of domesticating people, of making families into units of consumers.

It is therefore necessary to resituate emotional relationships within social institutions, and especially within the institution of marriage. From the sociologist's point of view, which I will adopt for the moment, marriage is a social institution that lays down structures in which children can be bred and brought up in security. Only recently has the companionship of the spouses been brought to the fore; previously, it was generally accepted that the aim of marriage was procreation. It could be that the view centered on the children had more wisdom in it than people care to admit today.

Marriage is an institution—in other words, a network of social roles and the necessary socioeconomic infrastructure. Its role in the family system seems to be to promote an institutional framework that provides security to new members of society. That is why marriage and the family system give a structure to a network of social roles and cultural patterns. Seen in this way, marriage is not primarily for companionship, but rather is primarily for children. Indeed, it is hard to see why an institution like marriage would be needed if it were only intended to promote companionship for adults. If, on the other hand, children have to be brought up, there is a certain amount of necessary security that can only be provided if not only the parents but also the rest of society work to maintain it. That is why marriage is linked to social organization and has political and economic ramifications. It is therefore important to understand the social reality of marriage and avoid reducing it to a couple's perception only.

The family system seems to have spawned two notions of the meaning of marriage in Western cultural traditions. The first, the more traditional, probably springs from agrarian culture. It says that children are the purpose of and reason for marriage. The second, which stresses the mutual development of the spouses, seems to be related to the economic and cultural changes brought about by, first, the creation of cities, and then by industrialization. As the places of work and residence became dissociated, as children became less a source of wealth and more an economic burden, and, finally, as the family came to be reduced more and more to the couple itself, so the emotional life of the couple came to seem more important. In advanced industrial societies, the economic importance of the family continues to decrease, and with it, the importance given to marriage (as in Sweden, where marriage is more and more a private affair between the spouses). In such a "privatized" society, ethical reflection tends to concentrate more on the couple and its life. However, I feel that the stress on children better reflects why marriage is an institution: the stability of marriage is surely necessary for children, whereas a couple can develop without it. For the couple, what is essential is the agreement and good will of the two persons concerned; for children, some kind of institution is always needed.

### Fidelity

To deal with the concept of fidelity, let us first compare faithfulness in friendship and in marriage. This question seems to have been for the most part avoided in ethics, where if fidelity in friendship is considered a virtue, it is often presented differently from fidelity in marriage, which is considered a duty.[21]

In both friendship and marriage, two people are committed to each other, and that commitment demands fidelity. In marriage, however, there is the special element of the sexual bond, which can bring about new life; thus, a child re-

---

21. Perhaps faithfulness in friendship has not been stressed as much by moralists because it does not have the same socioeconomic consequences.

quires the prior faithfulness of the couple, because the couple's love is needed to provide necessary emotional and material support. The specific kind of fidelity found in marriage seems to me to be related to this new life. Mutual faithfulness in marriage is certainly of great importance, but it is scarcely different from that found in friendship, if one does not take children into account. It is because of children that the couple finds itself committed to a long-term common purpose, and the faithfulness of husband and wife implies mutual aid so that their lives can be happy and fulfilled. The spouses' existences are locked together in their involvement in procreation, a process greater than themselves that affects their children and society. This explains why their faithfulness implies an effort to make each other's existence a happy one through all the ups and downs of life together.

Fidelity also gains importance by being presented in a more concrete way. Morals that are too centered on sexuality often forget the more general dimension of fidelity, which consists in assuming, to the best of one's ability, all the ties that have been created or accepted through the circumstances of life. In fact, concrete fidelities will always require that one be divided between diverse relations and competing loyalities. Fidelity to children will take away from time spent with the spouse; fidelity of the spouses will often conflict with their links with their own families. At the time of their engagement or marriage, the couple must also renegotiate the time and importance given to friends they had before their engagement. The spouses will also have to situate themselves regarding diverse affective relations present in their lives, as well as with regard to their professional obligations or the causes they are committed to. Thus, fidelity no longer appears as an abstract ideal or simply the opposite of adultery. It is a dynamic search for compromises between different human ties, often competing, none of which can be eliminated: ties to the partner, to the children, to friends, to members of one's social class, to colleagues and professional peers, and so on. These multiple human solidarities can sometimes be easily reconciled, but there are many cases where ties appear to conflict or even be incompatible. Therefore, simplistic solutions are not adequate. Compromises, or at least choices of lesser evils, must be made.

The question of fidelity leads us to the question of the indissolubility of marriage, which some cultural and religious traditions affirm. In those cultures in which women had scarcely any rights, Christian communities' defense of the indissolubility of marriage often caused men to go beyond economic or political considerations, or simple male selfishness, which tended to reduce women to mere objects of barter or child-bearing. The concept of indissolubility also reminded people that a relationship cannot be considered as not having occurred. This is true for any relationship, but had to be stressed in the case of marriage, because the socioeconomic implications are so great. Furthermore, indissolubility reminds us that it would be false to think that, just because one spouse does not fill what is "missing" in the heart of every human being, a new relationship—however exciting it may appear to be—will do so.[22] Finally, the symbolic and sacramental dimension that the Christian tradition has brought to marriage can affect the whole human community. It states that the institution of marriage (with all the economic, political, and cultural weight that it carries) can be lived and "read" in the story of God's love for his people; a creative, imaginative love, forgiving and refusing ever to become indifferent to the person once loved. Even for non-believers, the power of this symbolism can open up humanizing possibilities for conjugal life, as well as for any friendship.

22. Cf. L. Beirnaert, "L'indissolubilité du couple" *Etudes* no. 347 (July 1977), p. 7.

This declaration of the indissolubility of marriage, of course, never offers any simple solution to the complex problem of what to do when conjugal relations have deteriorated to the point where one wonders whether it is still appropriate for the couple to live together. Nor does it suggest what to do when there is no longer any life in common. In a Christian perspective it does state, however, that "remarriage" cannot be, in the same way, a sign and symbol of the love of God for his people, because the love of God never gives up. Nevertheless, for some people—including some Christians—such remarriage does seem to be a solution after the failure of the first marriage.[23]

The question of faithfulness, however, is more than just a question for the couple: parents alone are not enough for a family system. To bring children up properly, friends and schools are also needed. Furthermore, the parents' lives will not develop properly simply within the marital relationship; their emotional balance depends also on a large number of interactions with other people. Some partners consider their relationship as a necessary, but not a sufficient, condition for their emotional balance. Here again, there was a lot of wisdom in the tradition that stressed that the first aim of marriage was children, not the parents' development as human beings. Moreover, it is not very long since it was considered (no doubt wrongly in part) that marriage was too important a socioeconomic institution for its romantic aspects to be granted too much importance.

In the extended family, emotional development arose from a vast network of relationships, and not from the part-

---

23. From a Catholic point of view, it is important to consider that the Church does not recognize a sacrament (the visible sign of the love of God) in these remarriages. This does not mean that the Church judges decisions taken in all conscience by Christians. Some theologians even envisage the granting of a different kind of blessing to these Christians, just as Isaac did not hesitate giving benediction to Esau after he had blessed Jacob.

ner alone.[24] That is why it is scarcely surprising that today, also, in some situations, parents find much of their balance and happiness outside the couple. If, for example, one partner likes music very much while the other is not very interested in it, this need will undoubtedly not be satisfied within the couple. And it will certainly not be a matter of unfaithfulness to receive something outside the couple. On the contrary, it will be helpful and meaningful to the person who likes music and, consequently, to the other as well. What seems obvious when speaking about music may seem less so when emotional relationships are involved. It is, however, by no means certain that emotional balance and development must necessarily come from the couple and from the couple alone. Is it not possible, on the contrary, that a fully developed couple, really concerned with each other and their children, could be happy to see that their friends bring them some supplementary emotional fulfillment that they cannot give each other? Some people find part of their balance outside the couple; and sometimes it works out to the good of all concerned.

These days, the question has been raised whether, in such a situation, such emotional relationships should only be acceptable if no physical expression of affection takes place outside the couple. Some people wonder whether some physical affection may not sometimes be beneficial to

24. It would be worth thinking more about this tendency of our industrial society to attach so much importance to the couple that guilt feelings arise if a certain quality of relationship is not achieved. This demand did not exist in traditional society. Although the possibility of a profound relationship within the couple is doubtless worth stressing, the way it is virtually demanded in certain circles amounts almost to social oppression. The most important thing is probably to allow everybody to live, given each individual's personal and social limitations. Finally, it may be useful to realize that it was only relatively recently that the couple was given so much importance, no doubt in proportion to the enormous task imposed on the nuclear, privatized family.

the people concerned. The possibility of sexual relations is sometimes raised as well.[25]

I do not think philosophy or anthropology can provide clear answers to these delicate questions yet.[26] They are too close to the fringes of our culture. Many of our contemporaries are no longer satisfied with traditional reasoning, and yet it is important for those who take a certain distance from traditional values to know the consequences of leaving the framework of our traditional ethics. Such deviations carry with them the danger at least of disequilibrium, which some of them indeed do not escape.

### Conclusion

Rather than try to answer these difficult questions here, I shall only try to give a few indicators, which should not be neglected if one wants to think about these topics. However, I do not think that these indicators are in themselves decisive. In the end, people find themselves confronted with the guidelines left by our cultural or religious traditions, the collection of elements that can be analyzed, and what they see as their own personal path.

The first element I want to stress is that it is not appropriate to divide human beings into two parts, the body and the cultural, intellectual, or Platonic aspect. Most anthropologists and psychologists consider that we are our bodies and our bodies are us. That is why few of them believe today that there is a clear line between friendship and love; however, they provide little in the way of concrete indications, only

25. Concerning this difficult and ambiguous research in our culture, see Carl Rogers, *Becoming Partners: Marriage and Its Alternative* (Delta, 1973).

26. Christian traditions have had a clear stance on this point: love experienced as part of the covenant excludes extramarital relations.

the statement that any relationship is lived with the body. (But the question is, precisely how?)

But is it enough to use only physical or biological criteria? Many believe that such an approach is insufficient; apart from descriptions of material phenomena, however, it is hardly possible to draw a clear dividing line between biological and Platonic aspects. Moreover, the meaning of behavior can be very ambiguous. A smile to a person other than the spouse can sometimes signify as much of a threat to the family's security as a deep relationship that includes extramarital sexual relations. Finally, it is important to situate an experience in each individual's development. The experiences of psychologists and marriage counselors seem to show that too clear and definite a language on these questions can be risky in practice. Although they have often met cases in which adulterous relations have destroyed families, they have also met others in which people have achieved a certain liberation through such relations.

Of course, to notice this fact does not imply that one considers adultery as the normal path to liberation; it simply means noting that actual paths towards liberation are sometimes very different from what abstract principles dictate.

Can certain types of behavior have necessary meanings assigned to them? When this question is raised in an abstract way, anthropologists tend to make guarded answers. Actually, however, it seems clear that one cannot give just any meaning to a type of behavior. Human beings are involved in a biological and cultural evolution that at least partially predetermines the meaning of what they do. No doubt there are elements of the physical dimension that cannot be ignored without misrepresenting human relations; we cannot separate a relationship from its physical dimension. Nor can we modify at will those factors that determine our behavior and come from our culture and our education. The meanings of our sex life are obscure. When all is said and done, we do not know exactly what is implied by the taboos concerning bodies, in our own culture or in any other. Nor do we know precisely what our transgression of them would imply.[27] As the American psychologist Rollo May said, it may be that, in a culture in which sex and physical intimacy are taken too lightly, human relations lose their importance and their meaning, because, at least at first sight, they do not imply very much. Thus arises the danger of the relationship existing only for itself, which is why any kind of companionship or friendship, within or without marriage, should be related to real creativity—physical procreation or any other significant project.

The question of fidelity is also ambiguous. It is often inappropriately approached, as when it deals with a way of possessing people in the way that one possesses objects. Very often one feels ambiguity in language that reflects a background of personal property. We too often speak of "giving ourselves," of "possessing," when in fact we are talking about relations and their expression. Nor can we deny that the institution of marriage is often experienced as the private ownership of people's bodies and goods. That is why it is important to see faithfulness in marriage not primarily, or at least not solely, as a physical issue. After all, if adultery takes place, what counts is not only what happens with the individual involved, but particularly what might be wounded in the relationship with the spouse. It is not easy to describe what faithfulness implies, that is, the responsibilities to the spouse, to the children, and to many others.

Finally, it is important to stress an obvious point that is often neglected in the flood of lofty considerations: the danger of bringing a child into the world when there is no home to welcome it. All of the many other considerations that

---

27. It would be interesting to use cultural anthropological methods dealing with taboos and their violation to shed light on sexual ethics.

could be added would still not make it possible to completely encircle the question.[28] Indeed, very few people today feel that philosophical thought alone can do so. Some
people find practical answers in their own personal path or
in the guidelines of their religion, but that is not the concern
of this work on moral philosophy.

28. It might be useful to stress once again that any process of liberation requires a minimum amount of security, and therefore of cultural institutions.
Nothing could therefore be further from what has been described above than
this kind of sexual liberation, which exacerbates individualism and denies
any institutional or cultural restraints.

# PART THREE

# 8

# THE ETHICS OF COLLECTIVE ISSUES

### The reinterpretation of economic relations and structural ethics

Contemporary society is not content with reinterpreting the language of the body; it is also engaged in reinterpreting economic relations. Whereas the reinterpretation of body language is primarily concerned with private life, the reinterpretation of economic relations is related to work relations and to public life.

These two spheres, private and public, are themselves the product of the structure of industrial society, which tends to separate social problems from emotional problems, creating an ever-widening gap between professional or work life and private life. These two spheres are so distinct for many people that they cannot imagine that one could influ-

177

ence the other. This separation has an ideological function, however. For a long time, and still today, individual questions concerning private life have been used to "domesticate" the "people." Thus, the "good worker" behaves himself and looks after his private interests—in other words, finally, adopts the middle-class ethic in his working relations. That ethic is "private" (even when it is presented as "social"), and rejects any analysis of economic relations.

However, in an industrial society, the means of production and the resulting division of labor create areas of poverty and exploitation. After industrialization, social organization has changed, and the system of "social security" that the family agrarian society created has disappeared. In the past, and still today among the upper and middle classes, central ethical questions revolved around the family; but the family has become peripheral for many, while economic and work relations have become more and more central. Thus, in contrast to the situation prevalent in the Middle Ages, global economic relations and general questions of justice have become the subject of ethical reflections. This is what I call a reinterpretation of economic and working relations.

This reinterpretation is taking place in a different social class than the reinterpretation of the language of the body, which, because it depends on the existence of a private life separate from the productive life, particularly concerns those who have leisure time. The reinterpretation of economic languages, by contrast, finds its source in working peoples' experience of exploitation, and occurs as a result of tensions between the privileged and the dominated classes. Its location is in the lower and working classes, in the Third World, and among a few intellectuals who choose to be in solidarity with the oppressed. These social groups have a vested interest in naming and recognizing for what they are the relations of dominance, and in analyzing the structures of society. They thus go beyond individualism, to approach collective issues.

## The limitations of individual ethics

Ethics are concerned with human activities. Traditionally, moralists discuss motives, look for the meaning of actions, and judge the results. They lay down standards to regulate life. Such morals often appear external, outside concrete situations. When ethical precepts are presented as meaningful possibilities leading to liberation, they are no longer part of the ethics of proscriptions; rather, they institute a calling ethic.

Morals usually call on the individual's conscience. They are concerned with the individual's actions. Traditionally, the relationship between morals and the individual is extended into considerations of social ethics. Without looking into the specific nature of collective situations, people often apply a theory of action. The freedom of the agent is supposed to make the agent able to choose, to decide, which is what morals are about.

This individualistic approach to morals shows its inadequacies when it comes to appreciating the meaning of human actions. It is unaware of the collective dimension that surrounds the processes of liberation. It does not take into account the political, social, and economic structures, which guide the individual's action in society and over which the individual has no control. The outline of structural ethics that I present here tries to remedy this defect and to make clearer the social options of the free agents.

We see every day that individuals are caught up in situations where their own will has no effect. The social system, the economic organization, teaching programs, and so forth are all there to be adapted to. They are not the product of our choices and, individually, we are powerless to change them. What kinds of problems do these facts present us with? This can be appreciated with the help of the following story.[1]

A country village puts some meadows at the disposal of the villagers. Any farmer can lead his goats to browse there. The farmers take such advantage of this that soon the grass becomes scarce and the goats are starving. This overuse of the meadow raises the following dilemma: no shepherd has any interest in withdrawing his goats to let the others browse, but if no one withdraws his animals, the famine will get worse for all. This example illustrates the nature of a structural problem: it is caused, not by the action of one individual, but by a type of social organization, a problem that individual good will cannot solve. A structural problem can also be characterized by what kind of solution is appropriate. The solution cannot be an individual or a technical one,[2] but must involve a modification of the whole set of data concerned; in other words, we need a structural change. The solution requires a rethinking of the basic hypotheses according to which the problem arises. It is no longer a matter of solving a problem within a given social organization, but of changing that organization. We have looked at the problem of the village meadows, but the same kind of stories could be told about underdevelopment in a liberal economic framework.

We can now define structural ethics. Structural ethics concern the moral attitude to be adopted towards structural questions, that is to say, questions that cannot be answered properly within the framework in which they arise, but that

1. G. Hardin, *Population, Evolution and Birth Control* (San Francisco: Freeman, 1964), quoted from W. F. Lloyd, *Two Lectures on the Checks to Population* (Oxford University Press).

2. After Hardin, we call "technical" a solution that does not make a deep change in human values, ideas on morals, or the general way of life of the people concerned by the problem.

demand a change in the framework, a change in the system. Traditional morals, which judge collective situations through analogies with individual situations and acts, cannot cope with this type of problem. Ethical concepts as understood by traditional morals lose their relevance, making lucid moral judgment difficult. This is the case in dealing with the notions of offense or of guilt.

The notion of *offense* in morals concerns a person's responsibility. It presupposes, not powerlessness, but responsible freedom on the part of the subject. An offense is the action of a person that hurts another person. That is where the analogy between individual action and collective action stops short. Structural problems are cases in which individual freedom is not completely the cause of the offense, and in which the situation would be considered immoral if it were caused by the will of an individual.

For example, it is serious, and considered an offense, not to help one's neighbor in difficulties. But can the same individual who is responsible for his neighbor be held responsible for the trading structures and power relations that foster the exploitation of Third World peoples? At the collective, structural level, personal responsibility seems to be diluted. By adding together all the individual actions that make up the collective action, it would seem that one can find the individual nature of the action. Finally, everybody is responsible; in other words, nobody is.[3]

The notion of guilt is also linked to the sphere of individual action. People are aware of being guilty of acts or omissions that hurt others. An event that takes place in the

---

3. Some theologians introduce the idea of "collective sin" here. We should point out that traditional Christian morals have always recognized a type of "sin" that is objectively present, but that no living individual is responsible for, even if everyone participates in it: "original sin." When it is not used to generate apathy in regard to social structures, it can be a useful category for analyzing historical and societal evil.

network of a person's relationships affects that person, who accepts the responsibility for his behavior. But the guilt a person feels for participating in a collective action that is considered bad is much more uncertain. When Adam, in Genesis, is questioned by Yahweh, he shirks his responsibility: "It was not me, she told me to. . . ." If, at the level of individual behavior, such an excuse is already the spontaneous reaction, how much more justification can be found when dealing with collective actions? In collective cases, individuals seem to lose all control over the consequences of their actions.

When, at the interpersonal level, the feeling of guilt leads to reconciliation, atonement, or even expiation, it restores the relationship, which had been endangered or broken off. Guilt can be effective in its restoring role. But how can we repair the damage caused by structured forms of social oppression and of political domination? This question would be unanswerable if we did not try to situate it in the framework of structural ethics.

Guilt implies an understanding of what, because of our acts, we should take responsibility for. Without that, guilt has no foundations, and arouses neither emotions nor conscience. Faced with evil in which neither the initial agent nor potential liberation can be discerned, the individual moral conscience gets lost in perplexity. Even worse: since guilt is only felt in relation to individual situations, it often arouses responses that are inappropriate because they are geared to individual situations. Furthermore, guilt felt in relation to problems that one cannot solve leads, through frustration, to an opposite reaction. People refuse in the end to recognize questions that cause too much anxiety. This mechanism can be seen at work in relation to poverty in the Third World. Guilt-ridden individuals start by wanting to send cans of milk to the starving (or any other insufficient response). Then, tired of the insoluble problem, many no longer want to hear about it because, and not entirely without reason, "We can't do anything about it anyway, and in any case, it's not my fault."

What can be done when, apparently, nothing can be done? In the following sections, I offer an ethic for structural situations designed to answer this question.

## A Marxian approach to collective situations

The practice of studying the structural dimensions of actions goes back mainly to Marx. We must pay that tribute to him; he was one of the first people to show that poverty could not be lightened by mere charity, that is, by an individual action. Before Marx, society responded to the terrible collective problem of poverty more or less as follows. It was considered normal and natural that there should be rich and poor. Nature was like that, people thought, and it will never change. What was required was to start on the basis of an accepted structure and look for the best possible way of coming to terms with it. Rather than change the structures, then, people preferred to adapt to them through charity. Marx treated "all naturally evolved premises as the creations of hitherto existing men," which "strips them of their natural character and subjugates them to the power of united individuals."[4] Marx's method starts by refusing to consider the social structures of one's time as unchangeable and natural, which opened the way to what can be called structural ethics. His basic insight was that, where a superficial glance may see religion, politics, or economic activity, a deeper analysis may see an organized structure. From this insight, Marx constructed a new scientific paradigm for the study of social relations. It does not so much matter whether history has

4. Karl Marx, *The German Ideology*, Collected Works, Vol. 5 (New York: International Publishers, 1976), p. 81.

proved or disproved his analyses of "capital"; more important is that he opened up to analysis the crystallization of human relations in society and the tension between the individual and the community.

In Marx's opinion, all social institutions, such as religion, politics, and the economy, could be explained by relations of production in work. Indeed, "the division of labor"
also "implies the contradiction between the interests of the
separate individual or the individual family and the common interest of all individuals who have intercourse with
one another."[5] According to Marx, there is a relationship between the definition of roles at work and all social institutions. The only way to improve people's conditions is to go to
the heart of the problem: the division of labor and the ownership of private property, which are linked. Once again,
what is important is not whether he was right or wrong, but
rather his method. What he wanted was a study of the state of
the social structure as a whole and the real relations between
people, so that society could be changed in depth. He considered that, unless that study was done, any social compromises could be no more than palliatives. In other words, for
Marx, it is impossible to change society while leaving intact
the structures that cause the problems.

The Marxian approach to social change may not seem
very original. Nevertheless, it is important to examine his
premises: first, people must refuse to consider existing structures as "natural" or "self-evident"; second, any change presupposes a whole set of preliminary material conditions that
personal will alone is incapable of bringing about.

This perspective leads to a questioning of traditional
ethical values. Divine law, natural law, and moral imperatives are, for Marx, so many ways of avoiding the central
question: how to change the real world. As long as we re-

5. Ibid., p. 46.

main with these "idealistic" values, we are not facing up to the real historic tasks, that is, the tasks to be found in a particular new awareness at a particular moment in history, tasks that require a radical undertaking that is based, not on idealistic plans, but on concrete reality and practical conditions.

That is why, according to Marx, the way of bringing about structural changes would include several stages. The first is to understand the real relationships, as opposed to the imaginary or ideological ones, among people and between people and nature. The second stage is to choose a strategy for change that will not simply modify behavior, but really transform social structures and practical conditions. The third stage is to become involved in a practical way in the process of change, which, according to Marx, will necessarily be revolutionary.

### Examples of the field of application of the Marxian analysis

To clarify what is at stake from a structural point of view, we shall reconsider an example already mentioned.

Imagine a university in which it is felt that there is not enough community spirit; the students only seem interested in following their own personal aims. If the administration does not recognize the structural nature of this problem, it will attempt to remedy the problem by exhorting the students to have more community spirit. However, such exhortations will be to little avail if the lack of community spirit arises, not from the lack of good will on the part of the students, but from the structures of relationships in the institution and from the material conditions of life. A start should therefore be made by analyzing the situation. Such an analysis will show what the real relationships are between the students and the faculty and staff, together with a whole series of social and material relationships. The analysis should study the real relationships, not just the idealized super-structures. It will then be seen, for example, that the students' lack of community spirit is influenced, and perhaps even caused, by conditions such as the seating arrangements in lecture halls. It will also be noticed how competitive examinations can arouse relationships that eventually destroy any possibility of community spirit. The pressures working on the students will be revealed. Hence, to really change the situation, it is not sufficient to have everybody's good will; it is also necessary to change the material and social conditions in which human relations take place. That is where the choice of a strategy can be made. It is a matter of seeing, not only how individual behavior can be changed, but also the institutional structures within which this behavior takes place.

Once the analysis has been made, action must be taken. This kind of procedure would have some chance of changing reality, because the action taken would affect not only the individuals but also the structures at a collective level.

Later analyses after Marx have also revealed the specificity of structural problems. Some economic theories quite different from Marx's have described global phenomena, that is, phenomena that cannot be reduced to the sum of the individual acts underlying them. Keynesian macroeconomics is based on the recognition of these global effects. In its desire to operate at the level of large conglomerates—global production, global consumption, global savings, and so on—it finds itself proposing policies that are the opposite of what common sense would advise for individual behavior. Thus, during an economic depression, it seems reasonable to a company to decrease production. The order books empty, profits fall. The dangers of bankruptcy prompt it to cut its losses: production has to be trimmed to meet a weak, uncertain demand. What seems reasonable to the individual company, however, is not so on a broader scale. Keynes has shown that in a period of depression the state must take the responsibility of public expenditure and public works to create jobs and new incomes. By their cumulative effects, these affect the whole economic activity. The new incomes lead to new expenditure. This leads to a growth in the supply of products. The depression is checked, and there is an upturn in the economy. For this to happen, however, some intervention on the macroeconomic level, the structural level of the problem of a depression, has been necessary to overcome a crisis that individual entities were unable to handle.

In other fields, also, structural questions arise. Racism in the United States, for example, is a phenomenon partly beyond the individual will. Preaching against racism is not enough. The mechanisms of racism have to be analyzed. Economics as well as mentalities are at stake. Many interests are involved. Only structural changes will eradicate racism. The same is true of many problems, including those of foreign minorities, international trade relations, and monetary problems; only a global approach that goes beyond the power of good will exerted in a previously defined framework can hope to provide solutions.

Each structural problem requires its own analysis. As for individual moral action, one cannot give ready-made answers; we must be careful of facile schemes that are presented as the cure for all structural ills. That is perhaps the snag with over-simplified Marxism; social and economic reality has proved to be more complex than Marx imagined (as, indeed, physics has turned out to be more complex than Newton or Laplace thought). However, Marx's methods still remain valid: faced with a problem concerning the structural organizations of a society, it is important to analyze the real situation, to work out a strategy involving organized groups and not only individuals, and finally to act.

### Underlying assumptions for basic choices

In this introduction to structural ethics, I do not intend to go into the details of a series of concrete analyses. I will, however, provide a few keys to analyses, strategic choices, and goals for actions. Without going into the precise conditions determined by particular circumstances, it may be useful to examine the underlying ideologies of certain basic options in the analysis and choice of strategies and goals. I think that when it is a matter of analyzing social situations, people today mainly use one of two different models for interpretation, capitalism or socialism. I shall try to show how capitalist and socialist ideologies provide general frameworks within which particular analyses can be carried out. As far as strategy is concerned, these two ideologies oppose each other, and many choices of particular strategies are better understood when one realizes that a choice has to be made according to either a realistic approach or a utopian one. As for the determination of purposes for action, it is essential to decide whether greater importance will be given to the concrete results or to the intention. We shall speak of morals of responsibility or morals of conviction. In the following chapters, we shall examine these three pairs: Capitalism/Socialism; Realism/Utopia; Responsibility/Conviction. I do not claim that the ideological choices related to these pairs describe the main choices concerning analysis, strategy, and objectives. It would be wrong to try to systematize at this level. However, to a certain extent, when discussing structural changes today, one must always take a position in relation to these pairs. Study of them should, therefore, provide an analytical tool for understanding our sociocultural environment today.

# 9

# CAPITALISM AND SOCIALISM

Where structural problems are concerned, people are involved in collective actions that they do not master. Ethics is thus concerned with changing the structures. To put an end to injustices and to the evils that are contained within (and often part of) the system, the system itself must be tackled. Thus the ethical process implies an analysis followed by action. Analyzing a system means drawing a picture of its internal logic. This picture only reflects reality in a very abstract way, and it always depends on the point of view adopted and the methods of analysis used. Nevertheless, it should bring to light the structure's essential features.[1] Our

1. The term "structure" refers to the whole set of relations between the various elements of a unit. This is also the meaning of the term "system." We should also note that there is not only one capitalism or one socialism, but

question here is, what is the logic of capitalism and what is the logic of socialism?

## Capitalism

In capitalist ideology, people are considered producers and consumers. Nature is transformed in order to get out of it the goods people provide or buy. Economic activity is motivated by profits, and the search for maximum profits is regulated by the greatest possible difference between sales prices and costs of production.

The search for profit is a race in which, in principle, everybody is free to compete equally. Capitalism claims to be democratic, based on free competition and the private ownership of the means of production.

Competition is supposed to be fair and to stimulate economic development. The actual inequalities between people are not taken into consideration. They are "erased" in the analysis that the capitalist system makes of itself.

Capitalism made possible the development of the industrial society. Dynamic businessmen have constantly improved the quality of the means of production and of the products. Private ownership of the means of production and the power that that implies give those who possess them (and who are supposed to have acquired them by their ingenuity and their labor) the possibility of promoting production. Our society's relative prosperity certainly seems to be the favorable product of the capitalist system's performance. This performance, however, involves many external costs that business's accountants do not acknowledge, but that affect the situation of the workers and the living conditions of

---

several. Furthermore, it is needless to point out that when I speak of socialism here, I am not referring to any political party. In the same way, there is no purely capitalist or purely socialist society. The theoretical terms of "capitalism" and "socialism" only indicate tendencies.

everybody in an industrial society. These costs range from environmental pollution to occupational diseases, not to mention the discarding of unprofitable people (such as the old) and the exploitation of the Third World and of minorities.

Private ownership confers the power of management and decision to the owners of capital (or those to whom they delegate that power).[2] The workers take part in the company's activities as elements of production; they sell their strength to work. In exchange, they receive wages, but they are strictly confined to a performing role, without any share in their company's power or in the distribution of its profits.

This situation has always exposed workers to exploitation in many circumstances, and it still does. In order to live, they are forced to hire out their labor and accept the wages the company is willing to pay them. Free competition's so-called equal opportunity and economic democracy usually lead to a strict hierarchy. Power is concentrated in the hands of those who own or control the means of production.

The logic of capitalism also leads to other external costs that affect living conditions in capitalist society. As some say: "Capitalism also means a heart attack at forty." That doctor's opinion shows the dangerous way that an economic rationale can condition the way of life of a society. In the name of profit people hurry, worry, and are caught up in a rat race. The need for "more, ever faster" is an aggression on them as well as on their natural environment. Here we see the inherent contradiction in and essential flaw of capitalism: the search by everyone for profit (and the success of few) often works against finding happiness for everyone. The individualization of profits leads to the collectivization of losses. The myth that says that what is good for the companies is good

2. According to some economists, such as Galbraith, the power in companies no longer belongs to the owners of capital, but to experts and specialists, who form a technostructure capable of looking after the ever more complex management of companies.

for society mainly reflects the interests of some individuals, even if it is true that some kinds of "progress" do have beneficial spin-offs for the entire community.

Like any other ideology, the capitalist system structures social life according to its particular rationale. It has frames of reference that make it possible to understand social reality and therefore to make decisions within the social world. The rationale of capitalism is determined by profit and is centered on the market and productivity.[3] It is through criteria determined by these concepts that what is called "progress" will, in the end, be defined. Critics of the system who do not abide by these criteria (such as those who worry about old people or the quality of life) are often described as irrational. Indeed, they do not fit into the "rationale" of capitalism, which does not easily include such non-commercial commodities as health, education, culture, environment, old people, or the handicapped. This of course does not mean that a country run on capitalist principles will ignore social issues, but it does mean that, under the central rationale of the capitalist system, those problems are only secondary considerations and corrective elements in a logic that has its heart elsewhere. Moreover, when capitalism seeks to judge its performances, it uses criteria it has created itself (as, indeed, do practically all systems). Variables that do not enter into this "rationale" will be neglected. Thus, the capitalist system is much more likely to analyze trade reports than the restraints it brings about in people's lives or the free gifts between human beings. It cannot cope with the "accountancy" of pollution, families separated by their work, unemployment, or wars arising from the profit rationale.

3. It is important to distinguish between the organizing principles of a system and the social mechanics linked to them. Thus, the capitalist economy is organized according to the principle of the market. It is possible to conceive of an economy that keeps the mechanics of the market without being organized around it. Cf. on this subject D. Goulet, *The Uncertain Promise* (New York: IDOC/NA, 1977), pp. 229–32.

Finally, one evaluates capitalism very differently according to one's social standpoint. Those who benefit from the system—the members of the wealthy classes and, on the international level, the industrialized countries—will tend to appreciate a system that suits them. The unemployed or the exploited countries will see capitalism through other eyes. Furthermore, in those countries where capitalism is the rule, it is so well identified with the political-economic system that many people who see its flaws feel that by criticizing it they are sawing off the branch they are sitting on.

The most systematic criticisms of capitalism are provided by Marxism, which was built on that very criticism. In Marx's opinion, capitalism is the product of the division of labor in an industrial society, which itself is the product of new technologies. Through the division of labor, production was structured so that the owner of the means of production gained a lot of power over the worker, giving not much power in exchange. Private ownership of the means of production introduces relationships in which the owners dominate the others. In Marx's opinion, this basic situation leads to the logic of profit and capitalism as a whole. That is why he sees the abolition of the private ownership of the means of production as a necessary condition to a radical transformation of social relation. He aims at establishing a different relation between workers and the means of production.

This outline of capitalism is of course skeletal. Based on the notions of ownership of the means of production, of profit, and of production costs, it illustrates the inherent rationale of the system in a way that enables us to undertake the following analysis of socialism.

### Socialism

Beyond all the egalitarian Utopias, the prime objective of socialism is to prevent any one group or coalition of groups that constitutes a minority from leading and directing everybody's labor and profiting from it in a privileged way.

Socialism is not, therefore, inspired "in advance by doctrinal premises"; rather, it appears "at the end of the journey, as the result of the analysis of experiences." Starting with the experience of capitalist society and an analysis of its contradictions, socialism ends with its condemnation. The question is then raised: How can we replace that condemned society? Let André Jeanson reply with this description of the development of Christian Trade Unions in France. The workers' analysis of their conditions leads them to follow certain paths for research: "The economy must cease to be an instrument for profit for a minority at the great expense of the majority: hence the idea of the socialization of the means of production and exchange. The economy must be put to the service of the community and it must work consistently and efficiently: hence the idea of planning. The workers must be the masters of their working lives and, in more general terms, everybody should be responsible for their own life and that of the many communities in which they live: hence the idea of self-management. Only when these lines have been made clear can we situate them in a more global outlook and say: for us, that is what Socialism is all about." And for André Jeanson, this socialism means self-management that, among other characteristics, bestows "the right to think freely about Marxism just as about any other 'doctrine'" and to "accept as food for thought, the analyses, and concepts, from whatever source, which make it possible to answer the questions facing the human beings of our time." From these analyses, an economic rationale can be deduced.[4]

From the socialist's point of view, people are social animals before they are economic agents. Their economic role should be made part of a global plan: that of human life in

4. A. Jeanson in *Le Monde*, December 31, 1977, p. 2.

society. Equality is not a given fact biologically, economically, or culturally. On the contrary, the social experience is
one of relations of domination. Whereas capitalism is based
on the supposed freedom of all, socialism starts from the recognition of social restraints and limitations: organization,
working rhythm, privileges, and so forth. Change implies a
long job of equalizing the conditions of existence, which requires the imposition of constraints on individualistic desires to appropriate wealth. The community will not therefore leave complete freedom to individuals; rather, it will
control the means of production so that they cannot be used
to exploit or dominate other people, or to make private profits. This principle guides and defines the economic rationale
that is specifically socialist. Economic power will be considered as operating rationally when it conforms to the pri-
orities of the community. These choices meet the imperatives
of the direction chosen by society as a whole, and as such are
*political*.[5]

It is impossible in this brief outline to give a general description of all the different types of socialism, whether they
be theoretical (socialist ideologies) or applied (the various
socialist régimes). We must, however, outline a few socialist
ideologies, including the historically most important one,
Marxism.

We should first of all make a distinction between "utopian socialism" and "scientific socialism." Idealistic or utopian socialism envisions an egalitarian society, but gives little thought to the means of achieving such a society. This
type of socialism often attracts religiously minded people,
who find in it an expression of what they would like to see
but who do not go any further in their analysis. Such social-

5. It is interesting to compare political and economic relations in the two
systems. The socialist mode of production requires political primacy, while
capitalism tends (at least in theory) to keep politics out of the economic
sphere.

ists are often very "moralizing"; they reduce social questions to individual moral problems instead of seeing them as structural. Hence, some of them would say that people must first of all change their attitudes, stop being obsessed with profits, and change their hearts, and then everything will be better. Utopian socialism sees society as a structure that depends on material, economic, political, and cultural conditions. Therefore, it is hardly necessary for them to make deep analyses of society in order to change it. Extreme utopians act as if good will alone and individual conversions will suffice to change society, regardless of the society's structural conditions.

That is not at all the opinion of those who believe in "scientific" socialism. "Scientific" is an unfortunate term because, in a culture in which the myth that science is the foundation of everything reigns supreme, it seems to imply that it must have the ultimate answer to all problems. This is not, of course, the meaning of the term "scientific," even though a certain cult of science, lingering from Marx's time, does sometimes infest this trend in socialism. Rather, by scientific socialism, I mean an approach that considers society a subject that must be studied and understood theoretically in order to change it. To this extent, Marx, because he saw that economic, political, and ideological phenomena are related in an actual structure, and adopted a particular point of view in his analytical work, was truly one of the great founders of scientific disciplines. By presenting some theoretical concepts (such as the theory of evolution) and a point of view (a paradigm), Darwin made it possible for an approach to go further than had been possible with the empiricism that prevailed in his day; in the same way Marx made possible a new approach to social problems. By considering society as a topic for a structured study from a particular point of view (that of the exploited), by creating new, theoretically key concepts, Marx achieved an advance comparable to those of Newton or Copernicus or other fathers of scientific revolutions.[6]

### Class struggle or harmony?

A key concept of scientific socialism is "class struggle," which is central to the Marxist system and paradigm, but which is often ill-understood. It is neither a slogan for action nor an exhortation, but rather a theoretical concept, that is, a concept created for a better understanding of the phenomena analyzed, in preparation for action. The value of such a theoretical concept depends solely on how fertile it is in terms of understanding what is being studied and what actions should follow. Such a concept does not derive directly from experience, and it verifies itself only by its fertility in practice. This is just as true for the concept of mass in physics as it is for the concept of class struggle. To understand class struggle, a comparison might be useful: in 1970, in Vietnam, an observer would have been totally unable to understand people's behavior if he did not know the concept of "war" (or an equivalent concept). Without that concept, the behavior would appear absolutely irrational. On the other hand, everything changes with the application of that concept: a certain rationale appears that can henceforth be understood

6. On the concepts of scientific revolution and of paradigm, see T. Kuhn, *The Structure of Scientific Revolutions* (Chicago: University of Chicago Press, 1970). Saying Marxism is scientific in no way means that the method is perfect or that it never leads to error (it is indeed well known that all sciences contain many errors). It does mean that, by refusing to consider society as an object given once and for all, Marxism departs from empirical knowledge to go into a new relationship with its topic, with all the advantages and disadvantages of such a step. But this in no way implies that Marxism then becomes neutral or has no social standpoint. Indeed, the other scientific disciplines are not neutral either, despite the myth of objective science. Cf. my article in "Pratiques scientifiques et marxism," *La Revue Nouvelle* 68 (September 1978): 216–24.

(even though, in the light of other criteria, all wars are completely irrational). In the same way, by speaking about class
struggle, we imply that a whole rationale for behavior can be
revealed if we consider behavior as part of a struggle in
which the dominated groups try to defend themselves against
the groups that dominate and exploit them. Speaking about
class struggle, therefore, primarily means using a theoretical
concept that makes possible the understanding of certain social phenomena. The concept was not invented by Marx or
the left. Machiavelli, who has rarely been accused of being a
leftist, said that "in every republic, there are two different
dispositions, that of the populace and that of the upper class,
and that all legislation favorable to liberty is brought about
by the clash between them . . . good laws proceed from those
very tumults which many so inconsiderately condemn."[7] We
must take Machiavelli a step further, and say that the "dispositions" engaged in struggle are social classes.

In order to understand the meaning of the concept of social classes, other concepts have to be explained within the
dynamics of a socioeconomic analysis.[8] The starting point

7. *Discourses on the First Ten Books of Titus Livy*, I, 4: 2–4, in *The Discourses of Niccollò Machiavelli* (London: Routledge and Kegan, 1950).

8. According to Lenin, "Social class is the name given to large groups of human beings distinguished from one another by the place they occupy within
a system, historically defined, of social production, by their relations (usually fixed and regulated by law) with the means of production, their role in
the social organization of labor and, therefore, their ways of obtaining and
the size of their share in social wealth. Classes are groups of human beings,
one of which can appropriate the labor of another as a result of the difference between the places they occupy in a given regime of social economic." "La Grande Initiative," *Oeuvres Choisies*, Vol. II, part II (Moscow:
Editions en Langues Etrangères), p. 225. We should stress that the concept of
*class* cannot be understood except in relation to the organization of production in a given society. Many controversies exist between more or less orthodox Marxists about what classes and class relationships are. The most important element to understand as an analytical tool would seem to be that
the class relationship is not determined by subjective desires or the spon-

for this analysis shows that a society's modes of production (that is, how it organizes itself to produce what seems necessary for its subsistence) structure the society by laying down the production relationships (in an industrial society, an employment contract establishes different structures for workers and clerical staff; in a school, the means of production of knowledge establishes a distinction between teachers and pupils).[9] This structuring leads us to say that the members of the society are divided into classes. By classes, we mean, therefore, the distribution of the members of a society according to the structures brought about by the way goods are produced in that society. The members of each social class are therefore bound by common interests, which are determined, not by the desires of individuals, but by the individuals' place in the social structure, especially the structure of production. In the end, we speak of the class struggle as a concept that makes it easier to analyze social phenomena; that is, we affirm that these phenomena are better understood through the idea of class struggles and dominations than through more individualistic concepts.[10]

---

taneous and psychological wishes of people, but by the organization of society, which produces a certain number of goods; this organization introduces a certain number of social relationships independent of subjective points of view, such as master/slave, lord/serf, and employer/employee and employer/employee relationships.

9. Although industrialist/worker or professor/student conflicts are both brought about by production relations (on the one hand of material goods and on the other of diplomas), which themselves are determined by the actual organization of production, it would not be right to put the two conflicts in the same category. Moreover, Marxists recognize social classes in the first case, but not in the second. The means of extorting an increase in value that represents the economic basis of the social relationship between an industrialist and his workers is absent or at least very different in the professor/student case, where "orthodox" Marxism would speak of domination, not of exploitation. Further analysis might raise the question of whether there isn't real exploitation in the second case, in which the mechanics are certainly better.

10. The difference between a class interest and an individual interest can be

We can see in this way how the concept of class struggle forms the basis of a scientific approach to society, just as the concept of evolution formed the basis of a scientific study of the living species. We should also look at the social position of those who easily accept this concept and those who refuse it. In general, those who have a class interest in concealing inequalities and domination are the ones who refuse to make an analysis in terms of the class struggle.[11]

In our society, the analysis in terms of class struggle sits in opposition to an ideology that could be called the ideology of harmony, which represents society as a harmonious entity in which all problems can, with sufficient good will, be solved. Here, the world is seen as basically well-made, in that its structure is accepted. This ideology presupposes universal laws and an all-encompassing knowledge that can show where to look for solutions to questions. In this ideology, conflict situations are usually ignored. The oppressed are called the unfortunate; the exploited and the poor are the objects of charity.

According to this point of view, harmony arises from either a religious vision (in which God is the source of the "goodness" of the solutions) or a scientific one (in which the sciences show what needs to be done). In such an ideology, institutions are not usually called into question, because they are supposed to define ideal roles and behavior. It is, for

---

shown by the example of teachers. They may have an individual interest in not having rowdy classes, but this interest is not merely subjective, it is induced by the knowledge production structures of the school.

11. Another example may help here. During the wartime occupation of Belgium, to deny the existence of the Resistance, the Germans spoke either of bandits or irrational behavior. Here again we find a case in which the social situation of some people leads them to refuse the analysis made by others of the same phenomenon. In war, however, the phenomenon seems primarily to be related to the struggle for power, that is, to the political level, whereas the class struggle is linked to the economic level.

example, believed that the university or the factory will work well and in everybody's interest if everybody behaves properly. There is no place for conflict. It is always considered possible to find a "good" solution to any moral problem, be it abortion or labor-management relations. This idealistic outlook rejects the concept of class struggle. It refuses to believe that there is any deep-seated conflict within the very structures of the organization of society. By concealing these conflicts, it sides with the dominant group, the establishment, which generally perceives the world as harmoniously structured, precisely because it is the class that organized society. In the end, the ideology of harmony is an instrument of domination, because it implicitly defends the established order (or disorder). This ideology's logic of harmony is based on a benevolently organized world: it legitimizes paternalism, according to which some people claim the right to rule over others "for their own good."

Many Christians propagate this ideology of harmony, but this is not so strange when one looks at their social standpoints. Historically, this has given rise to a "religious socialism" that, while motivating people for a change in society, is not usually very effective, because it always aims to reconcile the irreconcilable in a universal harmony that conceals the reality of the conflicts. The tendency of some religious persons to over-value peace stems from this ideology. Finally, this ideology of harmony is often internalized by the privileged classes, especially the middle classes, which have great difficulty in perceiving the tensions of society. The members of these classes dodge the conflicts, even the most real ones, and often make a virtue out of their inability to live through them. They almost feel that it is a scandal to be involved in a conflict they did not choose. Hence they often value reconciliation at any price.

From our point of view, Marxian analysis is more a tool

for scientific analysis than an answer to all problems. Some groups, however, use this tool in a dogmatic way, as if Marxism were the answer to all social questions. This leads to Stalinist-style totalitarianism. This happens every time the relative nature of science is forgotten and a technocracy arises that, in the name of scientific knowledge, tries to answer political and human questions with the dogmatism of experts. Saying that Marxism is scientific therefore means—contrary to the myths about the meaning of "scientific"—that it is relative and that it should not be used to avoid questions about the meanings of one's choices.[12]

The rejection of centralized, dogmatic socialism leads many people to seek a socialism based on self-management, which enables people to make for themselves the decisions that concern them. Actually, self-management socialism characteristically joins the class struggle without reluctance on the side of the workers, but without becoming enclosed in the classic Marxist analysis of that struggle. As André Jeanson has pointed out, "Self-management raises again the problem of the very nature of democracy. Since 1789, the State has had the responsibility of ensuring equality, which it naturally tends to do by unification and uniformity. Thus we are easily lead down the path of State centralization, if not totalitarianism. Self-management presents the problem of equality within the themes of autonomy, diversity, and difference, and encourages people to struggle against all monopolies, whether they be political, economic, cultural or whatever. In the end, it sketches out a new outline for society."[13]

12. This point of view is the opposite of the one which, through scientific analysis, would like to determine the necessary evolution of society. Thus, Marxism as a theory of society would say what is going to happen. We do not need much history of philosophy to recognize here the scientism of Laplace and other positivists of Marx's time.

13. *Le Monde*, December 31, 1977, p. 2.

## Some limitations of socialist ideologies

Just as capitalism incurs social costs as a result of its internal logic, so socialism has its weaknesses. Measured against the criteria of capitalist rationale, it seems to lack efficiency. The practical application of the socialist ideology has usually led to rather deficient economic situations, at least when judged using the criteria of productivity and economic growth. Capitalists use the model of the free-enterprise economy of the United States to show that, however good the intentions of socialism, in the end capitalism brings greater happiness. They accuse socialist ideologies of ignoring one of humanity's greatest drives: aggressiveness and the desire to conquer.[14] They say that, by stressing the social aspect, socialism castrates the individual and diminishes the society's strength to survive. Above all, it downplays the search for individual gain, which capitalism considers the primary motivation for economic creativity. These gaps in socialism are all the more serious because the task of bringing about equal living conditions requires long-term planning. Without the initial motivation for economic activity, and uncertain of its results, socialism could lead to economic anarchy and the failure of its final plan. Adam Smith said an invisible hand leads individual capitalist interests towards the good of all. Under socialism, a visible hand works to impose the collective good. This hand may not always have enough fingers; nevertheless, we know that sometimes it can be an iron hand. Many people, at least those who enjoy much freedom in capitalist regimes (they constitute a minority) are afraid that socialism may not take people's rights into consideration (remembering the gulags).

14. It is interesting to note how, to legitimize this aggressiveness, modern ideologies use the languages of biology and ethology.

Generally speaking, the most severe criticism capitalism can make of socialism could be summed up as follows: "Socialism is very beautiful, but too idealistic and the results are often totalitarian." The capitalist prefers to take society as it is, call himself realistic, and work from human individualism and aggressiveness. The socialist, for his part, on the basis of his scientific analysis, counts on the future, on more humane people who will take other people into account. Historically, it is difficult to know which is more cruel, capitalist exploitation and imperialism or the excesses of socialism. It is, however, often the perpetual political conflict between realists and utopians that comes out in these discussions.

# 10

# REALISM OR UTOPIA?
# CONVICTION OR
# RESPONSIBILITY?

### Utopia versus realism

Structural ethics need analysis, but that is not all. Diagnosis is not enough; one has to think about the cure. How should one react? We must certainly take the specific aspects of a structural problem into account. Afterwards, two attitudes usually appear. Both attitudes are aware of what is at stake in the problem concerned, but one of them follows the equestrian's motto: "Throw your heart over the obstacle and your horse will follow." The other thinks that there is no point in taking such a risk if the horse has not been trained methodically to vault the obstacle. Utopia on the one hand, realism on the other, are not just questions of temperament. They represent two strategies that differ from each other in

**205**

the way they see time and history and in their sense of what is possible.

This is not a new choice. In *The Prince*, Machiavelli contrasts those who suggest all the qualities that a prince should have with the more realistic ones, who try to see what is in fact going to happen if the prince behaves in such and such a way. He concludes that, although ideally the prince should be a worthy and virtuous man, there is no point in his being so if that attitude leads to his being dethroned very rapidly. In contrast to such realists as Machiavelli, Freud, Bismarck, and Kissinger are those who can be called utopians, such as Thomas More, Erasmus, Gandhi, and Martin Luther King, Jr.[1] Put briefly, realists accept the world as they inherit it from the past and consider that they will not noticeably improve it, while utopians dream of a future world that they believe is worth working for.

### The realist

The realist looks at the world and finds that it is not perfect. People are not equals, they are unhappy; many problems are unsolvable. History does not seem to have any purpose and there is scarcely any point in working for a better world. People are what they always have been and what they always will be. The best one can hope for is to avoid too many catastrophes and do what one can to avoid the worst. For realists, people are aggressive animals who tend to attack each other and they will continue to do so. There is no real solution to that problem.

Some ideas about humanity, including those that look for greater democratization, seem dangerous to the realist,

1. The terms *utopian* and *Utopia* are not used here in the pejorative way that they are often used elsewhere; similarly, the term *realistic* does not have a purely positive meaning. In this book, these terms indicate an attitude toward politics, without any value judgment entering into it.

because they cannot be sure that a really democratic world could survive. It is always dangerous to aim too high, as doing so may bring about the opposite effects. Consequently, the realist defines policymaking as the art of the possible within clearly defined limits, which are set by the society's relations of strength and by a delicate balance between contradictory movements in society. Action demands prudence, knowing what one is doing. Progress must be gradual. Many small reforms added together are worth more than a "general revolution." Politics is the art of the possible, or, more precisely, the art of achieving what is least bad. It is also above all the art of maintaining oneself, of avoiding destruction in a badly designed world. That is why the rationale of the realist is defined in terms of law and order, which seem to be the guardians of a permanently threatened society. For the realist, liberty is more or less a secondary luxury, because too much of it will wreck the social organization, so that in the end people will be even less free. Deep down, the realist feels that society is threatened; it has no final purpose and the politicians constantly try to handle events with as little damage as they can, in order to survive. Just as realists distrust ideologies that they consider too idealistic, so they prefer technical solutions. Hence the ideology of the realist is often "technocratic"; that is, it entrusts political decisions to the conclusions of science and technology, avoiding the political dimension and not taking into account the presuppositions of science and technology.[2]

The political aim of the realist is first of all the protection of order, especially the protection of horizontal and vertical social relations. Sometimes realists will add secondary objectives. Humanitarian aims are not excluded, nor is the

2. Technocracy always supposes that science and technology are neutral, but all critics of modern sciences have shown that there are always some presuppositions and paradigms at the basis of any science and any technology, the ideological content of which affects the kind of solutions suggested.

desire to make as many people as possible share in the total welfare. Although realists give such aims a secondary place, it is not because they are bad or heartless. It is because, in their opinion, giving those aims priority would bring about the opposite effect. According to them, trying to be too good leads nowhere. Their means are naturally related to their general attitude toward politics. They live in a world of competition, conflict, force, and cunning. Finally, realists occupy a particular standpoint in society. Indeed, although they consider that the world is badly made, they nevertheless want to keep it as it is. There are very few realists—in my sense of the word—among the most exploited. After all, to be a realist, one has to have something to lose.

### The utopian

The utopian vision is completely different. Its basic hypothesis is that people can change, either because history has a predetermined purpose or because humanity is master of its destiny and can therefore achieve its own purposes. The utopians recognize human aggressiveness, but do not see it as finally determinant. People are aggressive, but they can get over it. It is, therefore, reasonable to hope for a better world. They recognize the material, economic, social, and cultural limits imposed by the past, but they do not feel bound by them. They have hope for the future. As Robert Kennedy said at his brother's funeral, there are people who look at the world and, seeing it badly made, wonder why, while others have a vision and wonder, why not? The first attitude represents that of the realist, while the second is that of the utopian, who has a dream to realize. Of course, there will be those who say, "You believe in Santa Claus!" But the utopian can point out that the unbelievable often comes true. Moreover, history has often shown the utopian to be more realistic than the realist. For example, at the end of the last century, when the *Rerum Novarum* encyclical was published, all the "realists" described the "unrealistic" nature of that encyclical in the liberal press, saying that it was contrary to economic reality. Today, however, the main objectives of that encyclical have not only been achieved, but surpassed.

Events of this nature make the utopians believe that they are right to hope and that, in the end, the strength of their hopes makes the world move forward. For them, politics is primarily the art of the imagination, which learns how to see things differently and to imagine ways of carrying them out on the basis of real analysis. It is easy to demonstrate to the realists that if we listened to them all the time, nothing would have been done. It takes people like Gandhi and Martin Luther King, people who believe in the possibility of change, to make change a fact. It also took all those unknown militant workers of the nineteenth century who struggled against all hope to contribute to the improvement in working conditions. Today, say the utopians, we need people who believe that our world can be more just.

For the utopian, society cannot be based solely on law and order; it must be open to the "general interest," and room must be made for a social ideal. The aims of its policies will be all those "humanitarian" elements that the realist can only envisage as secondary aims. Utopians seek, first of all, not the protection of an established order, but the participation of the greatest possible number in a better society. Their means must also participate in their aims. That is why the utopian often—but not always—uses what have been called non-violent techniques. Such techniques do not aim so much at condemning violence as at finding an alternative to it. Non-violence cannot be defined as the refusal of violent means alone. It implies the search for and application of methods and techniques that are really effective. Where necessary, recourse is taken to means of pressure and constraint that make the adversary give in and put an end to injustice.

Non-violence is not a technique of weakness, but of force;[3] it represents struggle before reconciliation.

When it comes to understanding society and establishing social theories, the realistic and utopian approaches are very different. The realistic perspective was expressed with great force by Hegel. In the preface to his *Philosophy of Law*, he refused to teach what the world should be like. He can only understand why the world is what it is, and, in his opinion, that is the job of the philosopher. For Hegel, philosophy and understanding (which in this book I call "analysis") always comes too late. It can only recognize reality, not produce it. The job of realism is to consider what is. If a theory actually goes beyond these limits, if it builds a world as it should be, then this world exists all right, but only in the theory, which is unsubstantial and can take on any aspect.[4] The utopian, by contrast, sees at the basis of his theory the inspiration of what is to be.

### Utopians or realists? Reformists or revolutionaries?

Utopian and realistic attitudes are subject to a number of criticisms. The realists are usually criticized for not wanting any changes; if the world had to wait for them, it would never improve. Nor do they offer liberation for people; they are devoted to an unjust established order. The utopians are criticized for their lack of realism. More precisely, it is suggested that utopians often neglect the relations of force.

---

3. Not all utopian policies make this link between ends and means. On the contrary, there are some for whom all means are good to achieve the target. As for non-violence, it would be wrong to believe that non-violent people count on the conversion of their opponents in order to achieve justice, or that it is a manifestation of love and not of force. It has political ambitions and is involved in all the dimensions of political struggle.

4. Cf. Hegel, *Grundlinien der Philosophie des Rechtes* (Meiner, 1821).

Being too preoccupied with their dreams, they do not always pay sufficient attention to the constraints inherited from the past, and they lack analytical rigor. They are also accused of sometimes encouraging a destructuration that makes their objectives less easy to achieve.

These criticisms may easily leave one perplexed. Each of these two attitudes has its limits and its problems, especially when they are caricatured. However, something of a solution may be found in the distinction between analysis and action. It seems to me that analyzing the situation as a realist would means automatically getting locked up in the past. After all, any analysis, even the most "scientific" one, depends on its underlying aims. In the analysis that is to determine the direction to be followed, it is important to aim at the society of one's dreams and imagination, rather than at the one that is simply handed down from the past. If our analysis is based on the organizational patterns we inherited from our history, we shall soon come to a technocratic conception of analysis and action, and uncriticized implicit factors can become determinant. But when it comes to acting, it is important to fit one's actions to real society—to the society that history has handed down to us. The action must fit society as it exists, not as we imagine it. But it is also important to be led by a dream of what could be, not just by what has been in the past.

We can illustrate these theoretical patterns with the concrete example of the university. Everybody knows the problems of the university: it promotes individualism and elitism, and it contributes to the maintenance of the existing class structure. The realists feel that these are minor inconveniences compared to what universities make possible, and consequently they give priority to maintaining the status quo, without taking our society's more or less latent aspirations into account. Utopians, by contrast, would like to see deep changes that would make the university more human and more democratic, not stuck in the structures that are so criticized. Realists act in such a way that, if there were no one else, there would never be any changes at the university. If the utopians followed their dreams and imagination, however, the university structures would probably disintegrate so quickly that there would soon be nothing left. Furthermore, the relations of strength are probably such that the utopians would probably even sooner be eliminated.[5] The solution I suggest is to analyze the situation as utopians, in order to show the gap between the university of today and the university of our dreams. This gap would determine a certain number of long-term objectives. Then, when it came to action, reference would not be made purely and simply to the imagination, because any reforms would have to take the relations of strength and the present structures of the university into account.

In other words, I suggest a revolutionary position as far as determining objectives is concerned, but I accept that, to a certain degree, any action is always reformist. A revolutionary situation is only reached when so many things have already been changed so that the social definition of reality has been modified. Revolutionary action thus would be action that changes the data in order to bring about objective changes toward the utopia aimed at. The difference between that and a reformist attitude would be the analysis, which determines different actions. Therefore I define *reform* as action that changes symptoms without aiming at structural modifications, and the *revolutionary approach* as action that aims at transforming the structure of the whole. This way of differentiating a revolutionary attitude from a reformist attitude is worth closely examining, because a revolutionary attitude

5. This was the criticism some people made of Allende: he failed to take the relationships of strength sufficiently into consideration, and he thereby neglected the economic, political, and ideological conditions of social change.

is often confused with violence or with a desire to seize power.

In addition, we must answer an objection often raised when social change is discussed: "What is the point," people ask, "of giving power to the dominated ones, if the final result is just to reverse roles?" That sort of change, of course, is only superficial; in my vocabulary it represents a reformist change, because it does not change the structures of oppression. To make this clearer, let us examine the micro-situation of a few people traveling together. If one of them has a car, this introduces into the social structure an objective relationship of domination, because one person has power over the others that is not reciprocal. This relationship in no way depends on personal intentions, but solely on the structure introduced by the ownership of a means of production (the production of transport). If the people get along well together, it may be that this relation of dominance hardly matters. If the non-owners rebel and take over the car, this would just represent a reversal of the roles of dominance, and the so-called revolution would be only a reform. If, however, by some means or other, the travelers managed to set up a new system of relations that prevented any one of them from having unreciprocated power over the others, then a revolutionary change would have been brought about, because the structure would have been modified.

This example shows clearly that a reformist change may improve the situation but leave the structure to go on creating dominations, whereas a "revolutionary" change produces a structure in which there are fewer relations of domination. Thus, in the southern United States in the years before the Civil War, any improvement in the lot of slaves was a reformist change; the abolition of slavery, since it modified the economic and political structures, represented a revolutionary change, at least from one point of view. A coup d'état that would have given the blacks power over the whites would only have been reformist, because it would have maintained racial domination.

Utopian and realistic attitudes both enter into consideration in any reflection about action, even if the ideological mechanisms may sometimes conceal their function. Indeed, a theory of society or of the world always presupposes a view of the future, a utopia. Any representation of the world is always a reflection of the way the world is structured, and is based on social vision, on presuppositions, on paradigms, on hopes. The view, therefore, depends on a picture of what the ideal society would be like, for both the realist and the utopian. Finally, the biggest difference between the two (and it is a very big one) is that the realist's thesis is usually produced in those circles that do not want deep social change, whereas the utopian's thesis is produced in circles that hold the opposite objective. Seen from a distance, the realist's thesis is just as unrealistic as the utopian's: indeed, history shows that the results are never what anyone had expected!

The attitudes of utopians and realists, as described above, could seem to be only the result of people's psychology. That is probably the way individualistic, psychology-based ethics would understand these questions. When, however, one looks at utopian and realistic themes in a particular society, structural analysis shows that their meaning changes according to the time and place at which they are uttered. In the end, they act as legitimizing ideologies for certain ways of solving political problems. This is why the choice is not so much one of individual psychology as one of social solidarity.

Any utopian or realistic language has a natural standpoint among social groups. The utopian thesis normally arises among social groups that, under the oppression of the established order, dream of another world. We can even say that such groups, with little to lose, can plan a future. The natural home of realism, however, is among those for whom the established order is "their order." It is therefore not surprising that many people who can be described as realists can be found close to the power centers (from Bismarck to Kissinger). Utopians, however, are often people who move among the under-privileged, and whose solidarity is bound with them (Gandhi, Martin Luther King, Jr., Illich). In order to understand the meaning of a utopian or realistic position, one has to look, therefore, not only at what is said, but also at how it fits into the social fabric and what it produces there. Seen in this way, it is no longer correct to say that these attitudes depend on psychological proclivities; they are social and political attitudes. It is impossible to describe either of them as good or bad, because they can only be understood in relation to their social function.

To penetrate more deeply, however, we must ask whether, behind these attitudes, there are not some radical differences concerning existence and its meaning for human beings. Indeed, inasmuch as the realist chooses according to the past, and feels that the same kind of human aggressiveness will go on being repeated in history, he takes up a position concerning human destiny. In the realist's opinion, human beings are determined by their past evolution—what is often called "human nature." For the utopian, by contrast, there is a gap between what human beings have been and what they could be like. They believe that man is an "unnatural animal" that can decide its future by making real choices. For the realist, the opposite is true. Behind these attitudes, there is perhaps a different kind of trust in the history of humankind. Perhaps the utopian attitude has a mystical dimension of hope for historical freedom that the realist's attitude lacks.

## Morals of responsibility or of conviction

The debate between utopianism and realism is also related to the ethics of responsibility and the ethics of conviction proposed by Max Weber (see Chapter 5). These two types of moral attitude concern the way of justifying an action. It could be useful to recall this theory here.

In *Stories of Florence*, Machiavelli describes the choice made by the people of Florence, who, he says, preferred the greatness of their city to the salvation of their souls. This choice shows what is at stake in the ethics of responsibility. In order to carry out their plans, they agreed to pay the price. They accepted responsibility for their choice and its consequences. The ethics of responsibility means knowing the price of one's action and being prepared to pay it. We must answer for the predictable consequences of our acts. That is the motto for an ethic of responsibility. It presupposes that no action will ever be completely satisfactory. It does not believe in a sort of pre-established harmony in the world, such that one could always act according to one's convictions.

The ethic of conviction is also aware of the price of action, but it refuses to pay it if that means sacrificing principles. Radical faithfulness to the precepts of an ethic (for example, those of the Beatitudes) is more important than seeking an objective that could require renouncing those precepts. The follower of an ethic of responsibility would, if necessary, accept the use of violence in order to establish peace. He knows the price of the aim. The follower of an ethic of conviction refuses that possibility. Convictions cannot be sacrificed without sacrificing the integrity of one's life.

Morals of conviction probably spring from a deeply individualistic perspective, and perhaps from a rather narcissistic point of view. Such morals do not easily accept the type of objectivity that the actual results of actions represent.

Moving toward an ethic of responsibility may represent a step forward for individuals who thus, in an act of trust and hope, say: "This is what I might make of my life." At this level, the rigor of the Weberian perspective, with its emphasis on the freedom of human choice, and the trust of the mystic converge.

# 11

# THE INDIVIDUAL AND
# STRUCTURAL QUESTIONS

We started off with a classical question: What meaning lies
behind human actions? This book has shown that it is impossible to speak about this seriously without taking cultural,
political, and economic conditioning into account. Speaking
of meaning in itself means speaking from some social standpoint, with some plans and aspirations in mind. We cannot
look at problems from a viewpoint outside history. Speaking
of ethics means considering oneself an agent within society.

The options one takes, then, do not float about in a world
of abstract and eternal values; we write our own story while
referring to those of others. And, whether we like it or not,
these stories speak to us of conflict situations. The categories
of oppressor and oppressed are essential for understanding
society, but we cannot reduce everything to that pattern. But
everything—consciousness, civil laws, our economic, politi-

cal, and ideological systems, and so forth—is impregnated with these fundamental conflicts.

That is why the category of liberation has a meaning. Not that it will ever be possible to say exactly what it consists of (no one ever knows exactly from what nor towards what one is liberated), but because individuals and communities talk to us about their liberation and thus arouse in us a feeling of hope vis-à-vis the oppressions and exploitations we can analyze.

Such liberation is both collective and individual, and so cannot be reduced to one of these two poles. Even emotional liberation and sexual morals, which seem to be primarily individual concerns, have a collective dimension, linked to the structures of society. And in the end, nothing absolves the individual from having to choose his solidarities.

To approach situations, an analysis is necessary. It must be as accurate as possible, especially by making its objectives and criteria clear so as to obtain a scientific validity. Nevertheless, an analysis always starts from presuppositions and a social standpoint; it could even be said that analysis stems from choices of solidarity more than it determines them. As such, analysis is essential to any action that gives greater importance to results than to mere sincerity.

Finally, there is that widespread feeling of our times: the impotence individuals feel when faced with collective and structural problems. Everything seems to combine to discourage people from changing the world and to make them accept the existing structures. And yet everybody must eventually take a position vis-a-vis these structures. This commitment is usually marked by choices of solidarities. These options, however, always depend on relative analyses, which are vulnerable to psychoanalytical, sociological, and ideological criticisms. Unless activists hide behind slogans or blindly give themselves up to scientific prejudices or totalitarian-style organizations, they know that nobody has the basic key to all analyses. It is, nevertheless, impossible not to be involved; even the silent majorities are. So what gives the activists their courage and élan? Is it an incredible naiveté, or a hope and trust that could perhaps be described as "mystical"? It is by confronting this mystery commitment, which reaches beyond analyses—which are always too brief or simplistic—beyond weariness and naive impulses, and beyond a vision of the world torn apart by critical thoughts, that this book ends.

As a comprehensive conclusion, I would like to examine some relationships between individual and structural ethics. This will lead us to study the role of moral norms as well as of attitudes toward structural questions, and finally to consider the source of the energy of those who face structural questions.

### Structural questions and ethical standards

I have shown above that precise ethical norms are usually inappropriate in structural issues. Inasmuch as they offer the individual possibilities of behavior that in the long run are ineffective or impossible, they engender feelings of guilt and often discourage further action.

In the areas we are concerned with, however, some general guidelines or ethical principles may be important insofar as they show directions to be followed. These precepts show, more than would detailed tactics for change, what can be considered as undesirable or desirable in the long term. Thus, if we take the problem of underdevelopment, which is a structural problem par excellence, ethical principles, by stating that it is undesirable that some nations should depend on others, could offer a Utopia, a vision that shows in which direction structures should be changed.

The affirmation of such general principles can sometimes represent a real step forward, since it makes it possible to discuss the Utopia they symbolize. Let us take an example from business ethics. It is generally accepted that ethical options can dictate the way in which money is spent, but the same is not true for judging the profitability of investments. Financiers often consider themselves responsible for giving part of their fortunes to social concerns or charities, but they rarely stop to think about the ethical choices involved in making that fortune. And yet the dividends from an investment in an international bank may come from the exploitation of the oppressed, such as when they come from South African industries that support apartheid. This is a structural problem, because any investor, however well-intentioned, eventually notices that the economic system is based on the exploitation of the poorest countries and individuals. The structural nature of the system often discourages people to such an extent that they eventually refuse to worry about how money is made. Some, however, follow an ethical principle in this, affirming that it is not right to ignore these issues. Such an ethical principle does not provide any particular strategy to promote the creation of a society with less or no exploitation. It does, however, present a utopian vision that can serve as a point of reference for change. Thus, some investors pay experts to study the social attitudes of companies they invest in. Then, at the corporation's annual meeting of stockholders, they question the management on their labor relations, and on other economic and social practices. While such actions are not likely to radically change the economic system, one may wonder if, little by little, they do not pave the way for more profound changes. That at least is how some ethical attitudes, such as the refusal to accept slavery, became established.

To put it briefly, such general ethical principles offer a utopian horizon for present-day society, and thereby contribute to change. We must, however, hold no illusions concerning their effects. They often remain ineffective unless a new relationship of force causes the partners to change their attitudes. Whether one considers decolonization or the oil crisis, it was only when the power relationship changed that the attitudes and ethical theses began to change.

### Individual ethics in structures

One difficulty with a structural view of ethics is that it has little correspondence with what the individuals involved in the problem perceive. The system of which one is a part resembles a constraint from which it is impossible to disentangle oneself. That is the situation of scientists who see their discoveries being used by others. Similarly, people in business know very well that, at least to a certain extent, they cannot escape engaging in some ambiguous practices. In some countries, for example, companies that systematically refuse to give bribes may find themselves without any orders—and, consequently, going bankrupt and leaving their workers unemployed. They are thus torn between the ethics of their convictions (their desire to be honest) and the ethics of responsibility (their desire to provide work for their employees and themselves). And that is only one example out of the many in which the individual feels caught in a system and driven back onto compromises.

One of three attitudes is usually adopted in such cases. The first is based on ethics of conviction: the individual decides that, whatever happens, honesty is essential and no compromises will be made with conscience. This honesty is determined by the ethical code of the society or group the individual lives in. The practical results of such honesty are usually tragic: contrary to what some people say, honesty does not always pay.

That explains why, in the face of such structural problems, some people abdicate and adopt an amoral attitude.

Thus, a large number of people in business eventually drop a lot of the standards that are offered to them and are content simply to avoid the too obviously "dishonest" acts. They adapt their behavior to social constraints. This attitude is characterized by the absence of any Utopia or hope to serve as a catalyst in their activities; they simply submit to the constraints of an unjust economic system and thus reinforce the system. Unfortunately, that is often the final attitude adopted by those who started with ethics of conviction; the impossible demands of their principles lead to moral indifference.

A third possible attitude starts from an analysis of the situation and assumes a Utopia. This analysis reveals differences between the compromises; some are necessary, but not all have the same effects. Some reinforce the system more than others. Analysis makes it possible to keep a direction, thanks to which one can hope to change the system rather than reinforce it. This attitude is a different path from either a rigid ethics of conviction or a moral indifference. It is doubtless in this way that one can find ethics of responsibility (and even an ethics of conviction, which, by principle, would also be concerned with the consequences of action).

### Obstacles to individual involvement at the structural level

The individual often feels lost in the face of a structural analysis of collective situations. A wide range of choices can be made, and none of them is absolutely clear; the relationships between an option and its consequences is not always obvious. Everything combines to make the individual hesitate and, in the end, become apathetic. First, there is the multiplicity of possible analyses. When, for example, one looks at the economic crisis, one can approach it from dozens of points of view. Which one should we choose? And having chosen, how do we know if we have made the right choice?

Indeed, any individual who is not completely blind or a fanatic perceives the relative nature of any analysis.

Second, there are the sociocultural determinisms; we are born and brought up in a given social situation and we all bear a series of marks of our social origins. Thus, those born in a privileged social class keep inside them a basic view of the world in which exploitation is not so much experienced as it is looked at from the outside. Even if such persons try hard to modify their view of the world, they are often caught acting or thinking like a lord or a bourgeois or a boss; ingrained habits die hard. Also, unless people have had training in social analysis and are activists, they never suspect to what extent a certain view of the world shows through their behavior.

Nothing is more difficult than to take a distance from one's social origins. Movements as unlike as the Chinese communist revolution and the growth of religious orders all show the same difficulty on this point. The communists have perceived how difficult it is for landowners to understand how a more just society can be organized. To fight this difficulty, they have used a whole series of self-criticism and brainwashing techniques to change individualistic mentalities and to help people see collective questions. What most Western observers see primarily—and, to a certain extent, rightly—as brainwashing is also an attempt to get people to perceive, or rather to experience, what exploitation is, and thus help them to adapt to a society that is defined in terms of a struggle against exploitation.

Interestingly, a similar institution is used in novitiates and other probationary periods of religious life. There, too, individuals are separated from the "world," that is, from the way in which society has taught them how to think and act, so that they can "identify elsewhere." Hence all those manipulatory techniques by which individuals are separated from their families and plunged into new situations through which, it is hoped, they will identify with the choices of Jesus Christ. Surely that is one of the main points behind giving up the "world" and taking the vow of poverty: to accept separation from one's "natural" inclinations in order to create a new inclination to follow the example of Jesus Christ by identifying with the rejected. These two examples show how difficult the task is; self-criticism does not always work, and, despite the novitiates, many monks and nuns remain fundamentally "of this world," that is, bound by their mentality and their culture to their social origins. And we know that in both cases attempts to change people's mentality have opened the way to abuses. There is a thin line between consciousness-raising and brainwashing or totalitarianism.

In addition to determinisms arising from social origins, economic and other constraints are also felt. Our society excels at enclosing individuals in subtle and varied pressures. The family as an institution, for example, is structured in such a way that a household has to "settle down"; one has to buy a house, pay the mortgage, enjoy a certain comfort, give the children only the best, and maintain one's social standing. By these little processes, a couple is quickly "reclaimed," and if they ever dream of leaving the establishment, they are soon "co-opted" back again. Professional structures operate in the same way. Our social organization, indeed, is characterized by the fact that individuals' professional success determines the mechanics of social control, which maintains order in society. Whether the individual is an executive in a company, a scientific researcher, a teacher, a politician, or a skilled worker, he knows that the only way is forward and up the social scale, never back down. This fact divides all these people in the name of "fair competition." Caught up in the rat race, individuals soon realize their limits. Even if they still want social change, they can soon only dream about it. The mechanics of social control are revealed when individuals have too much to lose if they do not behave as expected.[1]

In light of all these social controls, one can readily understand one of the fundamental requirements of any serious undertaking, be it religious or simply social: any such undertaking implies a lifestyle and a social status that leaves the individual free of too many social controls. These remarks make it easier to understand both the discipline imposed by communist parties and at least one of the dimensions of religious vows. Individuals have to put themselves in a situation in which they are less easily co-opted by the mechanics of social control. All those who wish to work for the liberation of people should think seriously about these control mechanisms and about how they intend to escape them.

Not only intellectuals and members of the middle class are easily co-opted in modern society; the workers, the lower class, and the poor are too, and sometimes more easily than the others. Although those who have fewer social privileges are more likely to suffer from oppression, and therefore be aware of the mechanics of exploitation, they are also more easily subjected to ideological domination. In a consumer society upheld by advertising, everybody internalizes the cultural models of production and consumption, which are at the heart of our social organization. Furthermore, in our industrialized countries, the workers are no longer simply an exploited class; they have become the middle class. But if, as we can say, "The workers here are not too badly off," it is because part of the exploitation has been exported to the devel-

---

1. We should point out here that the "system" that expects people to act "properly" is always ill-defined. It is not the princes, or the dominant groups alone; in a techno-scientific society, the entire social system, and not only the dominant minority, determines what should be done. In other words, to use one of Marcuse's expressions, we are in a prison in which the prisoners are also the wardens.

oping countries. That is why the workers of the industrialized world are not a proletariat that has nothing to lose from
a change in society. These workers have a vested interest in
seeing that the exploitation of the Third World, which gives
them a privileged situation, does not change.

Finally, among those elements that do not help individuals to seek a more just society, we should also mention that
each person has psychological limitations that, whatever
their origins, are an obstacle to a coherent commitment. Indeed, it is well known to what extent psychoanalysis can
cast suspicion over any radical involvement, by showing the
gap between what makes us act and our conscious motives.

### Choice, lifestyle, and solidarity

The ways people react to these obstacles to a commitment are many and varied. However, it seems to me that
some guidelines can be submitted that show what possibilities are open to individuals who would like to commit themselves to change in society. They stem from an analysis of the
whole set of constraints that can be discovered when people
are inspired by a Utopia of justice.

From a very general point of view, one can see the outlines of a basic option, which seems to stem from many philosophical, moral, and religious traditions. Depending on the
context, the terms of choice are presented in different ways
and with many nuances, but they all seem to be related to
one another. If one takes Hegel's point of view about the
master-slave dialectic, one may conclude that the slave is not
in the same position as his master relative to global history
and his own history. The master has to defend his interests,
whereas the slave, because of the condition of slavery, is
more aware of the human cost exacted in present historical
circumstances and is encouraged to think of new possibilities. Solidarity with the slave, then, is different from soli-

darity with the master. If, however, we see power as a structure spread throughout the whole set of social mechanisms, we once again find ourselves faced with a choice: throw in our lot with power, or rebel against it. In the first choice, we follow and accept the direction of the social system as a whole, while in the second choice, through well-defined actions, we try to allow something else to exist. From a Marxian point of view, the choice lies between being with the exploiter or with the exploited. For reasons related to the problem of the master-slave dialectic, Marx believed that in the end liberation will come for all humankind through the efforts of the exploited.

Finally, if we look at these choices from a Christian point of view, we find in the religious and theological traditions many relevant examples. St. John, for example, shows in his Gospel the conflict between the spirit of this world and the spirit of God. The story of the temptation in the desert speaks of the same choice: either bring people together by dominating them, filling them with awe, and feeding them, or bring them together by presenting oneself as vulnerable and as one of the poor and by wanting them to be free. Christian tradition has, moreover, represented these choices very clearly by showing the opposition between the spirit of Satan, seeking power, wealth, and honor, and the spirit of Jesus, who invites people to follow him in solidarity with the humble, the poor, and the oppressed.

To paraphrase Heidegger, it seems to me that all these traditions have basically the same meaning, even if they do not explicitly mention the same choices. Perhaps one role of the moralist, therefore, is to help people see the choices that are available to them. The moralist can help the calls that echo through history be heard and clarified. Then human beings must be left alone in the face of their freedom, their own existence, and their choices about what they are going to do with it.

It would, however, still be vain to talk about this fundamental choice without giving it a more precise meaning. How can the option that one wants to take be expressed in concrete terms? It would seem important to stress that, first, important decisions will be made through choices of environment and of lifestyle. It is usually by choosing a lifestyle that one commits oneself to a social reality, which leads to other options. It is also by avoiding some environments and by protecting one's social sphere and mentality that one impedes one's development. There are many choices of environment. For example, the place one chooses to live in. The middle classes learned that a long time ago, and are careful to live away from the poor; geographic distance protects social distance. Then there are the places one chooses to visit. Those who have chosen privilege will manage to visit a country without meeting its poor or exploited, and they will never have any contact with those who are fighting for the liberation of the oppressed. Then there are the social circles one chooses to belong to. A person whose friends are all intellectuals who hold liberal beliefs shows by that very fact where his options lie. Also important is the type of ideology one chooses to listen to. Some people only expose themselves to talk of harmony and reconciliation at any cost, while others can be found where conflicts and struggles for liberation are recognized. Finally, some people will be careful to be in touch with the struggles that are going on—strikes, the birth of new political regimes, experimental situations, and so forth. Others will prefer charitable activities, which do not call the existing structures into question. Some can be found where actions, choices, and even civil disobedience break the bonds of the existing order, while others will stay in the libraries. All these choices slowly shape a person's life-commitment.

Lifestyles are also important when talking about choices. If one does not accept, at least in certain aspects of one's life, some economic poverty, or at least a modest way of life, it is almost impossible not to be reclaimed by the control mechanisms of the consumer society. However, asceticism is not sufficient in itself; people can be ascetic and unselfish and still propagate values and acts that are contrary to their lifestyles and intentions (one may cite here the example of missionaries in colonial times). Even clothing is important; people who always dress like members of the privileged classes automatically cut themselves off from other social groups, and thus protect themselves from criticism.

Even these questions of choice of environment and lifestyle are still too general. They can only be given a meaning if one seeks greater detail. The choices that I have mentioned above constitute only a mytho-poetic form that lacks content for the poorest and most oppressed, unless a more precise analysis takes the risk of defining how it can be implemented in a given social and historical context. That is where, despite its limitations, a scientific analysis becomes important. It is also there, however, that many people, especially the privileged, dare not venture; they dare not choose which side they are on, with all the ambiguities and dangers that accompany that real choice. Because, to give a real meaning to these general choices, one must inevitably give up the illusion of solidarity with everybody's interests. For example, even though the interests of the industrialized world and the developing nations may coincide on certain points, they diverge on fundamental issues. There is, therefore, a choice to be made; even not to decide is to decide. When a strike breaks out, it is impossible to be on everybody's side; one has to choose one's solidarity.[2] And however unpleasant it may be for those who like to keep their hands clean, there is no such thing as neutrality.[3] The underlying ethical choices,

2. This does not mean that one cannot love those one is struggling aganst.

3. This expression, "who like to keep their hands clean," simultaneously

therefore, require both an analysis in terms of class interest and a choice. This choice will be particularly difficult for some, because it implies "betraying" their class interests. That is the situation for executives, teachers, and natives of industrialized countries when they choose to side with, respectively, workers, students, and Third World countries.

But the taking of sides, to be meaningful, demands that one live the real social practices of the side chosen. Only a constant and practical living out of one's basic options will take one beyond general declarations of a desire for solidarity. One must be able to refer to some support group at the grassroots level in which one can test one's options, question one's analyses, and study one's motivations—in other words, get practical criticism. Practical criticism, indeed, is not only the result of intellectual questioning; it stems from critical community (that is true for an intellectual work, the scientific community playing this role in science). Furthermore, these criticisms may be a way of testing motivations and practical applications. Insofar as such communities do not recreate oppressive practices within themselves, one may hope that they are working toward liberation. When, however, they reproduce social dominations, their members should do some self-criticism. In this way they fulfill the role of the critic, and one may hope that such self-criticism will prevent liberation struggles from ending up with gulags.

Choosing a support group, and thereby choosing a particular stand in society, is not easy for many people. Many, especially members of the intellectual and privileged classes, prefer to remain alone with their consciences, above any compromises caused by direct actions. They even try, sometimes, to describe their stand as "neutral," because it would

---

applies to those who, in the division of labor, are not on the side of manual workers, and those who, precisely because of their social situation, want to avoid making their choices and sympathies clear.

be based on scientific analysis. Sometimes, also, they hope to find in religion an uncompromised and neutral social position. In this way people dodge their responsibilities, because any action has its consequences in society, with the result that there is no such thing as social neutrality. Every theology, for example, also conveys some social ideology. That is why those who spurn solidarity with the dominant establishment must have roots in a support group that concentrates on analysis and action. Without this, any theoretical options taken will be vain.

### Energy and loss of energy among activists

Activists are those people who work hard to change society, especially those who attempt structural modifications. Such people often lose their enthusiasm and become discouraged. It is not unusual to see people who were ready to shake the world when they were young give up and become co-opted by the "system."

Several factors lead to this loss of energy. First of all, any structural analysis reveals a certain relativism that may easily lead to unconcern. Indeed, fanatics excepted, everyone knows that any analysis, including one's own, depends on a frame of reference or paradigm for "reading" the world. Thus, anyone who opposes the mechanisms of dominance found in relations between countries or between the sexes "reads" them through presuppositions. For all who are intellectually honest, one question often comes up: "After all, is my analysis correct?"

Aren't the others right? Who can tell a person, for example, if it is really right to say that the international economic system is the principle cause of underdevelopment? Shouldn't we really blame the presumed laziness or corruption of civil servants? And then, may not that person's analysis, based on a particular Utopia, produce results that are worse than the present evil? Activists who want to change the present university system, for example, may sometimes wonder whether the anxiety their activities produce may not do more harm than the established system. There are always people who stress their belief that such revolutionaries are only aggressive, harmful intruders, who may even be unbalanced.[4] It is also well known that many "revolutions" have in the end brought about few structural changes; what could be more like the czarist bureaucracy than the Soviet bureaucracy?

Further, the question always arises as to whether one is really doing anything. Activists cannot always be sure of the efficacy of their action; this is hard to accept when people find themselves poorly equipped to stand up against the "system" they are fighting. How much time seems to be "wasted" to earn a little democracy in a group, compared with the efficacy of the multinational companies, which move around easily in the society they are building in their own image. The activist is never sure of achieving anything.

Together with this feeling goes an awareness that analyses are always rather abstract and remain separate from the action. An engineer can see the results of his efforts in a bridge or a building; Martin Luther King could not see the results of his actions on the racist structures of American society. In the end, activists are always a bit cut off, because they are directing energies toward a society that does not yet exist.

Another cause of loss of energy is the tension caused by the "suspicious" character of any analysis. "Well integrated" people (especially the dominant groups) accept things for what they offer. The analysis, however, brings about suspicion. Is not such-and-such "aid" to developing countries

4. Without going as far as sending such people to psychiatric hospitals, our society often uses the "psychological argument" to discredit activists.

another form of exploitation? Is not such-and-such a right given to women just another way of keeping them in a male-dominated society? Although such analyses are very useful, they can become tiring; even the activist can want to live in a world where he can stop fretting over all these questions. This temptation is all the stronger when people believe—in my opinion, correctly—that trust is health-giving and widespread suspicion kills. Perhaps life can only be happy in a kind of abandonment to reality as it is experienced in society, to other people, and, for the religious person, to God. That is why the activist cannot easily find a balance between a simple life filled with trust and effective action.

In addition, psychology raises another suspicion about activism. How many times has a person thought he was saving the world, only to have psychological analysis show that it was just a struggle against parental or other fantasies? It is not always easy to make a clear distinction between personal problems and a desire for social change. All these ambiguities show that activists cannot persevere unless their action is based on deep-rooted beliefs and an attitude of acceptance, rather than simply on a rejection of present social structures. But how can one tell whether such acceptance is not an element arising from the process by which the activist may eventually be co-opted? That raises the question of the relationship between emotional life and activism. Unless a good balance is achieved, activism always looks like a headlong flight, or fanaticism. The key to this problem would seem to be an attitude of trust, which in Christian terms could be called justification through faith.

This attitude of justification through faith is the opposite of what is called justification through works or achievement. Those who seek justification through their achievements believe that, in order to be worthy of their existence, they must do worthwhile things. Such an attitude leads to anxiety, to wanting to know whether what is done is really worthwhile. By contrast, there are those who base their lives on a fundamental trust; knowing they are loved, they feel basically at ease. This fundamental trust in life (in those who love us and, for the believer, in God) enables those who have it to carry out a calm analysis of society and to act without too much anxiety. As long as people feel loved, they can make their social action less of a headlong flight; they can undertake it not because of unconscious personal needs, but because they want to. This basic attitude enables some people to be both confident and deeply involved in serious analyses. Furthermore, justification by faith gives those who experience it sufficient trust to be able to face their own ambiguities. Where those who justify themselves by their achievements are almost always obliged to maintain an image of themselves that seems valid to them, those who justify themselves by faith can discover without too much anxiety that they are part of an unjust society. They no longer find it necessary to moralize themselves and others. Perhaps there is in this a means of integrating action into the structural level, linked to a peace that accepts life simply. It is in such an attitude, which we could probably describe as mystical— whether believing or unbelieving does not matter—that it becomes possible for individuals to avoid being burned out by structural problems.

All this does not, however, answer the question of why some people—sometimes the most privileged ones—want to be in solidarity with the oppressed and to act accordingly. I do not think that there is any rational answer to that question, but it is a fact that there are always people who make this step. The impact of some prophets, religious or otherwise, should not be neglected; they have opened up such possibilities. But the mystery of such commitments nevertheless remains. Some people call it the action of the Spirit of

God. This mystery of human involvement is in any case witness to a liberating force in human society. It opens out hope
for human encounters without domination, and for reconciliation in forgiveness and tenderness.